HOW TO BECOME
YOUR OWN BEST SELF

HOW TO BECOME YOUR OWN BEST SELF

by Howard Grimes

Based on the Bi/Polar System
of
J. W. Thomas

WORD BOOKS
PUBLISHER
WACO, TEXAS

How to Become Your Own Best Self

ISBN 0-8499-0106-5

Library of Congress catalog card number: 78-59433

Printed in the United States of America

Contents

Acknowledgments

Many people have made this book possible. The basic ideas are those of Dr. J. W. Thomas, the originator of the innovative Bi/Polar System. Although we do not always express ourselves in the same words, I have tried to be faithful to his way of thinking about people and their growth. He read the manuscript and we conferred many times during its inception and development. Because I agree with his ideas, have profited personally from them, and have presented them in many seminars, I did not find it difficult to utilize his understandings.

I am also indebted to many people—almost fifty—with whom I have worked in seminars and other ways, and those who provided written, oral, and taped statements. The identity of such persons is not given in most instances, but without their help the book could not have been written in its present form.

I also want to thank my wife, Johnnie Marie Grimes, who served as a sounding board for the book and long before I wrote it helped me in learning to live with people who are different. Two typists also were of great help: Mrs. Marlene Bassham who typed an earlier version and Mrs. Anne Norris who typed the present version. My colleague, Richard T. Murray, read parts of the manuscript, and both he and my other colleague, C. Wayne Banks, prepared the way for me to accept Bi/Polar ideas as we worked together for many years.

The Bi/Polar chart on page 58 is based on a more elaborate one in Bi/Polar: A Positive Way of Understanding, by J. W. Thomas (Richardson, Texas: BI/POLAR, Inc., 1978), and is used by permission.

H. G.

Introduction

I am delighted that Howard Grimes has written this book. Bi/Polar needs to be presented in a religious context and Dr. Grimes is eminently qualified to do it. He is a professional Christian educator (he has a Ph.D. in religious education and for many years has been a professor of Christian Education at Perkins School of Theology.) He is also a certified instructor and supervisor of Bi/Polar Seminars. And finally, he is an accomplished writer. He put all three resources to work and produced this book— an accurate and lucid presentation of Bi/Polar from a religious point of view.

It hasn't been easy. Not only did he have to contend with me, the originator, looking over his shoulder, but he wrote it when a number of changes in the Bi/Polar system were taking place. No sooner would he complete a draft of his manuscript than here would come a radical new development requiring major surgery on what he had already written. Right after he completed his first draft in early 1975, we had significant new insights into how the strengths relate to each other. We also found a better way to pictorially present the eight patterns of strengths. As a result, he had to rewrite major portions of what he had already written. By the time he had finished this rewrite in the early part of 1977, additional new and important clarifying concepts had come along and needed to be a part of the book. Not only that, but, in consultation with his publisher, he had decided to make it a much more "personal" book. All this brought about the third and final rewrite of the manuscript. Now, we have the result—an up-to-date presentation of Bi/Polar from a personal and religious point of view.

Dr. Grimes says it differently than I do and places emphasis at different points. For example, I tend to emphasize the separate, independent, and distinct *individual;* whereas, Dr. Grimes tends to emphasize the *relationship* between individuals. This doesn't make either of us "right" or "wrong." It is simply an expression of two different tendencies within two different people. In the final analysis, we both adhere to a common point of view— being a *separate individual* and being in *relationship with others* are of equal value and *both* are required to produce an authentic human being.

In reading his manuscript, I have been tempted many times to redo what he has written and put it in my own words. I am glad to report that I have refrained from doing this and limited my reactions to that of a consultant on the accuracy of the concepts. I have not tampered with his way of expressing himself. This is a real advantage for the reader. What Dr. Grimes has written here *complements* rather than duplicates what I have written.

In spite of the fact that Dr. Grimes' "style" is very much different from my own, he faithfully presents the fundamental philosophies and concepts of the Bi/Polar system. Our objectives are the same—to help people understand themselves in terms of their strengths, understand others in terms of their strengths, and through these understandings develop skill in their communications and relationships.

Although this is unquestionably a "religious" book, I

would be disappointed if being labeled as such would have the effect of causing a less "religiously oriented" person to put the book down and not read it. Anyone who has a desire to better understand himself, other people, and their relationships can profit from reading this book. It has my unqualified recommendation.

J. W. THOMAS
Richardson, Texas

Part I

Discovering Your

Strengths

–1–

Born to Grow

In my mid-fifties I discovered a new way of understanding myself and other people. I regret that this discovery came so late in my life. Had it happened earlier, I would have been saved from false hopes about my career, and I would have been freed to be more fully my own self. Who knows? Perhaps if I had truly understood who I was, some of those hopes might have been realized, for this new resource also helped me to understand how I could draw upon both greater and lesser strengths for a more fully actualized life.

In a sense this book is a testimony and a witness to my discovery. It is an attempt to share this tool—not as a panacea for all your problems but as a means of coping with life so that you can become your own best self.

Although I do not always use religious language in discussing my discoveries, this book is a religious book. It is an affirmation of the belief that God is the Creator and that his creation is good; that humanity abuses that creation and therefore, in religious language, sins; but that God is still the Lord of creation and enables persons to become their best selves when they are true to themselves, to the Creator, and to one another. The basic idea *can* be understood within traditional Christian or Jewish theological frameworks, or without such frames of reference. You are invited to use its insights within your own commitments and loyalties, therefore, to actualize the potential God has placed within you in the creation process.

I want to make clear, moreover, that what I will be talking about is not a substitute for religious commitment and faith. Rather, it is a plan for you to use within the motivating and enabling power of your faith. There are many other books which talk directly about personal faith—for example, those of Keith Miller (such as *The Taste of New Wine* and *The Becomers*). I consider what I am writing about in this book as a supplement to and not a substitute for what Miller says. We will be helping you identify the way you can work creatively within your faith commitment.

This, I think, is what Miller himself has in mind when he writes that "conversion is only a 'beginning' and not an 'arrival.' The convert has just been freed to start actualizing the gifts and potentialities which have always been inherent in his life." [1]

Your Gifts and Potentialities

What this book does, then, is to help you identify and learn to use "the gifts and potentialities" that are within you. Wherever you are on your life's pilgrimage, this is a possibility. If you are older, as I was when I encountered the insights on which this book is based, your resistance to new patterns of using your gifts and potentialities may be stronger than if you are younger and more flexible. You can still change, however. There is a dangerous half-truth in the maxim, "You can't teach an old dog new tricks." Maybe you cannot do this to a dog, but you, as a child of God, can learn new "tricks," regardless of your age. To put it

[1] Keith Miller, *The Becomers* (Waco, Texas: Word Book Publishers, 1973), pp. 11–12.

more accurately, you can learn to use your gifts more creatively.

Another way of talking about your gifts and potentialities is to call them "strengths." Throughout the pages that follow, we will be concerned with strengths. We will say little about your weaknesses, believing that the way to deal with weaknesses is to use strengths in a more creative manner. The emphasis is on learning to cope with life and its opportunities, as well as its problems.

Some of the crises of life come from within. These are the crises about which Gail Sheehy writes in her book *Passages*.[2] All of us are familiar with the problems involved in growing from childhood to adolescence and eventually to adulthood. But we are less aware of the fact that such inner turmoil and conflict continue into adulthood. We will not attempt to identify these inner crises, only assume that they do in fact occur.

We are much more aware of the problems which arise from outside us. People fail us; circumstances at times seem to overcome us; we have problems in relating to other people. At times these outer forces surface in more dramatic forms: the death of a friend or relative, the loss of a job, disappointment when a child does not turn out as we had hoped. And there are always the daily demands of living and working with people—in the home, at work, in church or synagogue, in our social life.

Born to Grow

In spite of these problems, however—those within us and those outside us—we were born to become persons who can cope with life creatively. What do we mean by "creatively"? The simplest way of putting it is that we are made to work out relationships with other people which are helpful to us and to them. In the process of coping with

---

[2] Gail Sheehy, *Passages: Predictable Crises of Adult Life* (New York: E. P. Dutton & Co., Inc., 1974, 1976).

problems and with people, we move toward becoming the person we were meant to be.

To put it another way, we are born to grow. This is most easily seen in physical growth. Children grow larger and stronger if they are provided with the kinds of food that the body needs. They also grow mentally partly as a result of gaining maturity, partly as a result of intellectual stimulation. If they are not provided with adequate food and mental encouragement, their growth will be stunted.

People also grow emotionally. They learn how to accept and give love, how to express and control anger, how to use fear when it is needed to avoid danger, and how to control fear so that it will not become a crippling emotion.

We also sometimes speak of psychic growth. "Psychic" comes from the Greek word that means, among other things, "life." Religion speaks of spiritual growth. Our concern is with psychic or spiritual growth—the growth of the whole person in relation to his/her self, to others, and to God. This kind of growth involves both thinking and feeling.

The Bible is clear that we are born for this kind of growth. Genesis speaks of persons being made "in the image of God" (Genesis 1:27). Psalm 8 speaks of our being made "little less than God." However far we may fall short of reaching our potential, we are born to grow toward mature manhood and womanhood.

The desire to become a more adequate person is, in fact, one of the distinguishing marks of all persons. Unlike the other creatures of the earth, people are able to decide, to make choices, to become, to will to grow toward the realization of their God-given potentialities. Animals can be *trained*; human beings can be *educated*. We can will to be or not to be, to grow or not to grow.

Yet it is not simply a matter of willing to do better: how many New Year's resolutions last for more than a few days? Trying a little harder *may* help, but it is not enough. In the early twentieth century a Frenchman, Emile Coué, believed that this was all that was needed. He developed a self-help formula that consisted of the repetition of the words, "Every day in every way, I am growing better and better."

What we need is a plan that utilizes our God-given potentialities for becoming more adequate persons. Such a plan must include at least four parts: a way toward greater and deeper self-understanding that leads to healthy self-esteem; a means of understanding other people that contributes to our appreciation of them in their diversity; help in personal growth within our own basic faith commitment; and, as the outcome of the first three, assistance in developing more creative relationships. In subsequent chapters we will look at these four "steps"—both in terms of some fairly simple but fundamental ideas and in relation to actual people through case studies that in some instances employ the words of the people involved.

It is such a plan that I discovered and that I now want to share with you.

Discussion and Activity Guide

1. In what way or ways would you like to become a more self-fulfilled and self-actualized person?

2. Write out two or three goals you now want to accomplish with regard to your growth. Put your statement away and look at it again only after you have completed the reading of the book.

–2–

Two Kinds of People

The first fact I learned which increased my self-understanding was that I am stronger in thinking than in risking. It was also an important discovery for me to recognize and accept the fact that other people do not react to life in the same way I do. The distinction between thinking and risking is the first decision you need to make concerning *your* strengths. This chapter is designed to help you decide in which of these areas you are stronger, as the first step toward greater self-understanding.

Because I am stronger in thinking, my natural inclination is to begin by defining the two terms, thinking and risking. Since I have also learned that my *natural* way of doing things is not always the *best* way, I will not follow the path of least resistance. Rather, I want to tell you the story of how a psychologist developed a new understanding of personality. This will, I believe, allow you either to *think* or *risk* (feel) your way toward your first step in a deeper understanding of yourself and others.

In 1955, J. W. Thomas, with a newly earned doctorate in psychology, began his work as a psychological consultant to business. As he went about helping business executives become more effective in their work, his creative and innovative mind began to analyze and draw conclusions from his experiences. During the next ten years he continued to reflect on the facts that emerged from the hundreds of interviews he conducted, all with men in business.

Out of the crucible of experience was born the understanding of life on which this book is based. Dr. Thomas eventually adopted a name to fit his conclusions—the Bi/ Polar System. He has made many refinements in his thinking during subsequent years as he and more than 100 specially trained women and men have used the system in a variety of settings. These situations have involved people, both women and men, from many walks of life. Most of these people have gone through a nine-hour seminar led either by Dr. Thomas or a certified instructor. In fact, some 15,000 persons have done so.

Two Kinds of People

Underlying all other facets of the system is Dr. Thomas's first discovery during those early years—that there were two kinds of company presidents. One kind he identified as the dynamic, assertive, enthusiastic entrepreneur—the person we sometimes call the "go-getter." The other is the stable, cautious, steady organizer—the person we sometimes describe as being "like the Rock of Gibraltar." The first takes risks easily without always doing adequate thinking. The second thinks and organizes but is not always willing to take the risks necessary to venture forward into new fields of endeavor.

The president of one insurance company with which Dr. Thomas worked is an example of the first kind—the dynamic actionist. In the company's first seven years it grew rapidly. Enthusiasm, confidence, and optimism were clearly evident in the organization. The volume of business continued to increase, but losses also mounted. The company lived from one crisis to another; the president made decisions quickly and there was little planning. Decisions often turned out to be mistakes which brought harm to the company. The company was moving, but it was not going anywhere.

A second company was older. A dynamic leader had begun this oil company during an oil boom in the 1920s. The firm prospered, but then it began to falter. At this point the owner's son, a stable organizer, stepped in as president and reorganized the company.

When Dr. Thomas was called in as consultant, the company, under the leadership of the owner's son, had become so stable that there was little life in it. Company executives spent most of their time making one exhaustive study after another, perfecting procedures, and carrying through other kinds of "red tape." The company was no longer moving forward, and its profits had fallen dramatically. The firm had become so preoccupied with its inner structures that no one was taking the risk of moving out into new ventures.

There were two possibilities open to each of these presidents. One was to draw upon his own opposite strength (thinking or risking) to do what was needed. One of the presidents tried this, but his efforts were relatively ineffective. Although this alternative is often followed by individuals in their day-to-day life, there is another possibility, especially for an organization.

The alternative is to draw upon another person with the opposite strength for help, and this is what both presidents did. The first secured a person with great stability strengths and made him Executive Vice President with authority to reorganize the company's operating procedures. The second placed a dynamic person in charge of each of the five divisions of the company and gave him authority to move the division off dead-center. This meant that both companies had in maximum degree the strengths of risking (dynamism) and thinking (stability).[1]

[1] These examples are from Dr. Thomas's *Your Personal Growth* (New York: Frederick Fell, Inc., 1971), pp. 24–33. The book is now out-of-print.

The way in which these two company presidents faced life represents a basic difference in people. Some tend to *feel their way* through life and move into action without fully thinking through what needs to be done. Others tend to *think their way* through life, to organize life and take care of details, and may not move into action at all or act too slowly and too late.

To put it more exactly, some people *lead* with feeling and others *lead* with thinking. Those who lead with thinking are more stable and less dynamic. Those who lead with feeling are more dynamic and less stable.

Thinking and Risking

As I began to understand myself with Dr. Thomas's help, I was able to accept what I had known but had not been able either to express or affirm: namely, that I tend to think a long time and finally act. Although I am not in business, my acting sometimes came too late for optimum effectiveness. I learned the real meaning of the maximum, "Not to decide *is* to decide."

I also came to understand that my wife is naturally the other kind of person. She tends to act quickly and to think afterwards. This had made for both interesting possibilities and frustrating problems in our marriage. We had been aware of the problems and to some extent the possibilities, but we had not always been as tolerant of one another as we might have been. I came to see that she often makes a decision before I have thought long enough to decide what the question is!

I do not mean to insinuate that thinking and risking are not both a part of the make-up of every human being. Of course they are! Nor do I mean to imply that those stronger in thinking do not have deep feelings and are not able to act decisively and when necessary even quickly. Similarly, I do not mean that those stronger in risking do not think. To be a human being is to think.

What no one had told me, however, is that it is *natural*

for some people to be stronger in thinking and for others to be stronger in feeling, and that coping with life involves learning to use the two strengths in creative interaction. This was what the Bi/Polar System did for me, and it freed me to *know* myself and to *be* myself.

This freedom came partly through the realization that neither of these human qualities is more valuable than the other. I suppose that if someone had asked me up to the time I began to think in Bi/Polar terms, I would have said that thinking is more important than feeling. Our heritage from the Greeks has exalted reason, and much of my basic response to life had been formed by this tradition. Further, thinking is my natural way of responding to life, as I have already observed.

I was not unaware of, nor did I fail to appreciate, the fact that the Hebrew-Christian tradition is based more on a story than on a philosophy. It is a story that begins with Abraham and for the Christian comes to its fulfillment in Jesus Christ. A story embodies feelings fully as much as reason. In fact, the Hebrew-Christian tradition may be more feeling-oriented than thinking-oriented. At least there is a strong component of feeling in it. It was rather that my natural inclination and my participation in an academic community for many years had made me more acutely aware of the distinctive human quality of reason. The Bi/Polar System, along with other personal experiences, gradually made me much more aware of the equal importance of these two human qualities.

Nor had anyone helped me see that thinking and feeling are more than *qualities* of persons. They are also *strengths*. That is, they are qualities that can be used to the full, partially used, or even misused. And they are not fully and creatively used until they are understood to be two poles of human strengths, to be used in relation to one another.

The *strength* based on the ability to think we will call

Bi/Polar Thinking. As we will see in detail later, it consists of two kinds, the Practical and the Theoretical. Practical Thinking deals with things as they are—with facts, data, plans. Theoretical Thinking deals with things as they might be—with ideas, possibilities, theories. The two together are based on the human quality of rationality, or the ability to think and use our minds. Bi/Polar Thinking *strength* produces both stability and the creative understanding of reality, the ability to identify and analyze a problem and to imagine a possible solution. We will usually use the briefer term "Thinking" to designate this strength.

The *strength* derived from the ability to feel we will call Bi/Polar Risking. Although it is based on emotion and feeling, it is not *just* feeling. Risking is the strength that grows out of our ability to feel deeply, to move forward even when we are not sure *how* to move, to act even when the way is not clearly seen. Although risking is not the same as faith, it is this strength which the New Testament Letter to the Hebrews describes with regard to Abraham: "By faith Abraham obeyed when he was called to go out to a place which he was to receive as an inheritance; and he went out, not knowing where he was to go" (Hebrews 11:8).

Risking strength also involves two poles, Dependent Risking and Independent Risking. Abraham's act included both of these poles—his dependence on God and his willingness to act individually on that dependence. Dependent Risking strength frees us to draw from others and let others draw on us. Independent Risking strength makes it possible for us to move out on our own, risking ourselves in freedom and intentionality. Bi/Polar Risking strength produces creative confidence in ourselves and others, or interdependence. The contrast between Thinking and Risking can be shown most easily by noting basic differences in how people face life.

Three Illustrations

Dr. J. W. Thomas,[2] the originator of the Bi/ Polar System, is a creative and innovative thinker. He enjoys nothing more than spending many hours thinking through the meaning and implications of the system which he began. His initial period of thought, during which the basic design of the system was forged, lasted for ten years. During this time he tested and retested his major ideas in his work as a management consultant. The use of the system was restricted almost solely to what he could himself do during this period.

By the end of this decade he had concluded that the system was sufficiently developed for others to begin to use it. At this time he had the good fortune to meet Richard T. Murray, Director of Continuing Education at Perkins School of Theology, Southern Methodist University, in Dallas, Texas. Murray, a dynamic actionist, was relatively new in his job and was searching for ideas that he could use in his program of continuing education with the clergy. Convinced that it could provide help for church people, he "bought" the system on the basis of his intuition. He enlisted several of his colleagues, including myself, in learning the system so that they could use it in what were then called "growth seminars" (more recently "Bi/Polar Seminars").

Within the next ten years, Murray not only incorporated the seminars into his own program, which was expanding greatly; he also began introducing others to the system. In 1972 the first exposure to the system beyond the Southwest came when he persuaded a national meeting of Christian educators to offer two brief seminars as

---

[2] Real names are used in this illustration. In most others, names and circumstances are changed for the sake of anonymity.

a part of their program. During ensuing years it was largely Murray's dynamic leadership which helped spread the ideas to various parts of the United States.

In the meantime, as the demand for seminars increased, Thomas's wife Jane became the stabilizing force which kept the enterprise on an even course. Neither Thomas, the innovative thinker, nor Murray, the dynamic actionist, was interested in the detailed work involved in setting up seminars, coding the inventory forms which participants complete, and handling the other details of keeping the seminars organized and supplied with material. Jane Thomas is also stronger in Thinking, but, unlike her husband, is more practical than theoretical. Always in the background, Mrs. Thomas has been the one who has provided the organizing ability to make the seminar operation possible.

In this illustration we meet two persons stronger in Thinking—Thomas, the theoretical thinker who produces the ideas of the Bi/Polar System, and Mrs. Thomas, the practical thinker whose work in the background keeps the seminars organized. Neither has the Risking strength which made it possible for Murray, as only part of his total professional responsibility, to lead in the establishing of a network of certified instructors who now hold seminars in many parts of the United States and Canada.

In another situation three teaching colleagues plan and teach courses as a team. One is stronger in Thinking, more theoretical than practical. It is he who ordinarily brings to a planning meeting of the group the ideas for a course. These ideas are usually somewhat different from former plans for the same course, a source of irritation to a second colleague who is more practical and does not always see the necessity of making the changes. This same colleague is independently dynamic and often disagrees with his more theoretical colleague about the way to begin a course. While the first finds it natural to begin by setting forth the basic ideas of the course, the second prefers to begin with some experience which plunges the students immediately into dealing with the course material. As an action-oriented risker, this is his natural way of teaching.

The third colleague is also stronger in Risking but in a dependent, relational rather than an independent, self-confident manner. When the other two cannot agree, or when the first becomes defensive concerning his ideas, the third steps in and becomes the reconciler. He is more interested in the dynamics of relationships than in either the ideas of his first colleague or the assertive attitude toward these ideas of the second. It is he who is often the catalyst in resolving the disagreements between the other two.

In this second illustration we see a person stronger in Thinking who likes to think through and plan a course, usually in a logical and idea-centered manner. The second teacher, stronger in Independent Risking, wants to move ahead and get things done, with as much experience-centered teaching and practice involved in the course as possible. The third, also stronger in Risking but with a relational slant, is willing to accept the ideas of either or both of his colleagues and is most interested that the three maintain a good working relationship. He therefore becomes the reconciler when the other two disagree.

In the interchange each stimulates the other to use both his greater and lesser strengths. That is, the theoretical thinker encourages his more practical colleagues toward better theory as well as toward a more constructive use of his experiential approach to teaching. The independent, practical risker helps his more theoretical colleague in his theoretical thinking and also toward a more dynamic approach in the teaching situation. The relational risker in turn acts as a catalyst in making his other two colleagues more sensitive to the people involved in the course when it is taught.

A third case involves three young people who have a new but flourishing small business enterprise. The first, John, is dynamic, talkative, enterprising, a leader, high in Independent Risking. The second, Harold, is a stable thinker—quiet, a good student in high school and college, level-headed. The third, Jean, is also higher in Risking but more relational than independent. She is charming, a good conversationalist, practical, a good salesperson in a "soft-sell" manner, able to relate well to everyone. As a team the three have succeeded where any one alone could hardly have survived in the highly competitive market which they serve. Harold provides the ideas and caution; John furnishes the dynamic "push"; and Jean brings to the enterprise a degree of relational dynamism which neither of the others have.

Basic Assumptions

These three cases illustrate a fact of human experience: namely, that people bring different strengths (or gifts) to a relationship or a situation. Modern technology may treat people like a set of holes on a computer card or a social security number, but this is not what people are. They have their own individuality, and they can make significant contributions to life if they are freed to be themselves and given an opportunity to express their true selves.

The first basic difference in people concerns whether their greater strength lies in Thinking or Risking. Before I move on to some practical help to guide you in making this decision about yourself, I want to state five basic propositions about the two strengths.

1. *All of us have both Thinking strength and Risking strength.*

It is obvious that we both *think* and *feel.* What is not always obvious is that these are not only qualities; they are also *strengths* to be used deliberately. Dr. Thomas, though higher in Thinking, used his Risking strength when he approached Murray to try to interest him in the Bi/Polar System. Murray, though higher in Risking, used his Thinking strength to plan how to promote the Bi/Polar System which he had accepted on the intuition that it was good.

2. *In all of us either Thinking or Risking is greater.*

No one is perfectly balanced with regard to these two—that is an attribute of God alone. God is perfect; human beings are imperfect. And perhaps the greatest sin of all is to claim to be greater than we are, even to pretend to be God. The sin of Adam and Eve was their pretension to be something they were not: "For God knows," said the serpent, "that when you eat of it [the fruit] your eyes will be opened, and you will be like God . . ." (Genesis 3:5). Part of what it means to be human is to accept our finiteness, our limited nature, our "lop-sidedness."

JW appears to many people to be as strong in Risking as in Thinking. In his profession he has learned to move decisively and dynamically. But when he begins to tell you how he struggled in order to act so commandingly, you begin to realize the price he has paid to do so. In vivid detail he recounts the plans he makes to take control of a situation that is out of hand, and there is no longer any question concerning where his major strength lies—in Bi/Polar Thinking.

3. *Thinking and Risking are of equal importance.*

All of our cases have illustrated this proposition. In all where more than one person was involved, it is clear that both Thinking and Risking were necessary to make an enterprise go.

This is not to say that all situations demand the same amount of both. In an emergency we need to move out—to risk—without thinking of all the consequences. Our action will be wiser, however, if we have planned ahead for such an emergency. Rescuing a drowning person requires quick acting, but action based on impulse alone, rather than knowledge also, may prove fatal to both persons. *Knowing* it is better to use something that floats rather than ourselves as the object a drowning person grasps, we are more likely to be successful in our efforts to rescue the person.

What others expect of us may also make it difficult for us to express our natural strength.

MJ is a young woman whose Bi/Polar inventory clearly showed her to be independently dynamic, stronger in Risking. Her actions during the seminar confirmed the results of the inventory. This revelation was troubling to her, however, for she is from an ethnic group which expects its female members to be quiet and submissive. She is neither quiet nor submissive! Further, her husband is a clergyman, and the usual expectation of ministers' wives is that they will remain in the background. Her natural tendency is to want to be "up front." MJ has not solved the conflict between her natural self and the role her subculture expects her to play, but it has been of help to her to realize that she must find acceptable ways of expressing her stronger Risking strength.

4. *Well-rounded persons learn to use both their Thinking and Risking strengths in a creative manner.*

Most of the cases thus far cited have indicated one way in which this is done: to work with a person with a complementary strength. The other way—one which will be our primary concern in later chapters—is the plan which JW followed. His first inclination is to find others who will supply the strength which he lacks, but he has found that this is not always possible. In most of life we must learn to utilize our greater strength to help us use our lesser. This is what JW has done, and in so doing he *appears to be* much more dynamically independent than it is his natural inclination to be.

5. *The first step in learning to cope with life is to accept who we were born to be.*

Socrates said, "Know thyself." Jesus took the Jewish injunction and made it into his second "great commandment," "You shall love your neighbor *as yourself.*" Present-day psychologists are unanimous in affirming the necessity of self-acceptance, self-affirmation, and self-esteem. Accepting ourselves is the beginning of personal wisdom and of the ability to cope creatively with life. It is not enough, of course, but it *is* the initial step. And this chapter is designed to help you take the first step in such self-affirmation.

Making a Choice

I hope by this time you have already begun to see yourself as stronger in either Thinking or Risking. To provide additional data, I suggest six typical reactions of the two kinds of people.

1. *Those higher in Thinking strength enjoy the thought world of the mind—either facts and data, or ideas and possibilities, or both. They are more likely to enjoy thinking about and planning than the actual doing.*

Those higher in Risking strength, on the other hand, enjoy activity, either with people or as an individual exercising his/her own personhood. They quickly move beyond thought to action. The doing may either be with others or alone.

2. *Those who lead with Thinking often refrain from sharing their thoughts in a meeting until they have con-*

sidered the options available and the qualifications which
must be made with regard to any statement.

Those who lead with Risking strength often speak early
in a meeting, without clarifying their thoughts in their
own minds. Both tend to become irritated with the behavior of their opposite.

3. *Those with greater Thinking strength usually have
problems in making decisions. They often are so concerned
about having all the facts that they postpone a decision
too long, and they may find it difficult to decide at all.*

Those with greater Risking strength, however, tend to
make decisions quickly, often based on intuition rather
than facts. They may even appear to be impulsive, and perhaps they are. Decisions are not difficult for them, and they
sometimes make snap judgments and think afterwards.

4. *Those who lead with Thinking usually move with caution.*

Those who lead with Risking are often adventuresome
and are willing to take risks.

5. *Those whose greater strength is Thinking usually
make commitments slowly. They finally give themselves to
something but only after weighing the facts and the ideas
involved.*

Those whose greater strength is Risking often commit
themselves rather quickly. If they are higher in Dependent
Risking, their commitments may be formed by the influences of a group. However, if they are higher in Independent Risking, they may make commitments without group
influence and stay with their commitment even when
others question it.

6. *Those higher in Thinking strength usually find traditional education to their liking. They respond positively
to courses that are arranged logically, with a progression
from one set of facts or ideas to another.*

Those higher in Risking strength often have problems
with formal schooling. They may find experiences beyond
the classroom more to their taste and learn best from real

experiences. They often find an action/reflection model of learning more compatible with their natural response to life.

In the light of these differences, you are now ready to answer five key questions as you seek to move toward greater self-understanding. Read them and make an "a" or "b" choice quickly. In instances where you do not find a clear decision easy, ask yourself which you are more inclined to be or to do.

1. Do you make decisions (a) slowly _____ or (b) quickly _____?
2. Are you (a) naturally cautious _____ or (b) naturally adventuresome _____?
3. Do you (a) usually plan with care _____ or (b) move into action rather quickly _____?
4. Are you (a) more of a planner _____ or (b) a doer _____?
5. (a) Do you tend to be fairly reserved? _____ (b) Or are you naturally outgoing _____?

Now count the "a's," and the "b's." If your "a's" clearly outnumber the "b's," you see yourself as stronger in Thinking. If the "b's" clearly outnumber the "a's," you see yourself as higher in Risking. If you are not sure, go back and read the illustrations in the chapter and see with which persons in those cases you identify most readily.

Summary

The basic question in this chapter has been how you face life and its problems and opportunities. I have made it clear that I do so *in most instances* by means of my Thinking strength. In other words, I *lead* with my Thinking, though in each of the five questions I could find exceptions.

I *usually* make decisions slowly and often painfully, but *sometimes* I do so quickly. Usually when I make them quickly it is due to a period of preparation which preceded the decision time.

My wife *usually* makes decisions quickly, however. (In adjusting to my tendency, she has disciplined herself to move more slowly, especially when the decision affects me personally.) This is not to say that decisions are not sometimes difficult for her; rather, she prefers to make them and get them over with, while I fret away valuable time that could be spent more creatively.

I am naturally cautious. I put money into savings accounts, for example. My wife is adventuresome; she loves to invest in stocks.

I usually plan with care, and when I do not I usually regret it. At this point my wife does not altogether fit the pattern of the risker, for her life has been spent professionally in enterprises which required her to plan carefully. Yet her natural inclination is otherwise. For example, we were recently asked to make a contribution (larger than we would normally have made) to a project of human development carried out in another country. Her response was, "Let's do it!" Mine was to check our resources, think about it, and eventually make the contribution.

I enjoy planning but dread having to do something (like teaching a course). My wife struggles with planning, but enjoys the doing.

In a social setting where my wife and I are present, I usually speak sparingly. It is she who must carry the weight of the conversation, which she does with skill. I am frightened by persons in authority; she is completely at home with them.

There are exceptions, as I have indicated. But it has been of comfort and help to me to recognize what my natural ways of reacting are and therefore to be better prepared to work toward a more creative use of my Risking strength in relation to my Thinking strength.

I hope this book will do the same for you regardless of where your greater strength lies, in Thinking or in Risking.

Discussion and Activity Guide

The questions, suggestions for discussion, and plans for activity in this and the following chapters can often be done best with one or more other people who are also reading the book. If you are working alone, check yourself by rereading the relevant material in the chapter.

1. Who is the originator of the Bi/Polar System on which this book is based?

2. List the characteristics of Bi/Polar Thinking and Bi/Polar Risking. Look at the two lists. With which one do you identify most readily as the stronger in your natural or preferred way of negotiating life?

3. Go back through the five statements with "a" and "b" choices. Make a tentative decision concerning where your greater strength lies, in either Thinking or Risking, and write your choice on a sheet of paper. Keep this sheet with the book as you read further.

4. How would you react to life differently if your greater strength were the opposite from the one you have chosen?

—3—

Two Kinds of Thinking

Some time ago I began to have trouble starting the engine of my automobile. At first I heard a timid whir when I turned on the ignition key, and then nothing at all. These were the facts of the case: the car would not start, and the reason was that the ignition system was not supplying the current needed to set the motor in motion.

I immediately developed a theory: my battery was worn out, even though it was only a year old. So I acted on my theory and took the car to the garage where I had bought the battery. I gave the mechanic the facts and my theory. He accepted my theory long enough to test the battery, which he found to be sound. Here was an additional fact, and it required another theory.

Why was the battery not staying charged? It could be the alternator, but hopefully not, for alternators are expensive. The mechanic had another theory: it might be the regulator. He tested his theory, and it turned out to be right. He replaced the regulator, charged the battery, and my problem was solved.

This simple illustration describes a process which is as common as eating and sleeping: the human mind moving back and forth between facts and theories. It is the think-

ing process which is a part of the natural endowment of
every normal human being. It is one of the God-given
abilities which distinguishes the human from other creatures.

Facts and Theories

The two kinds of thinking—one related to facts and the
other to theories—also provide the basis for the second
pair of strengths with which we are concerned in this book.
The purposes of this chapter are to identify these two
strengths, to help you determine whether you are stronger
in Practical or Theoretical Thinking, and to help you use
the two more creatively.

These two ways of thinking are human attributes, but
they are more than that. They are also *strengths*. Therefore, the concern of this chapter is more than the *identification* of your greater strength in this pair. It also begins
to show you how you can express *both* of the strengths
more completely in the life process. We are especially interested in how the two can be *used together* to help us
cope with life. When they are used effectively in relation
to one another, we have become *creative thinkers*.

But before we can exercise our Thinking strength to the
full, we must identify which one is stronger in our
make-up. This self-knowledge is the first step toward becoming more creative in our thinking.

Practical Thinking

What is Practical Thinking? The key words in identifying this strength are *facts, data, reality, planning, application*. When I think about things *as they are*, I am being a
practical thinker. If I ask the questions, "Will it work?"
and "How does it work?"—I am asking practical questions.

Practical Thinking is a simple fact of everyday experience. We cannot avoid it if we are to negotiate life. But

the question is, do we really use our Practical Thinking *strength* as completely as we might? It is only when we use that strength to analyze a situation or a problem in its fullness that we are doing so. If we stop short of such a careful analysis, we are only partially using the strength.

For example, I am not "mechanically minded," whatever that may mean. Anything more complex than replacing a light bulb or checking the oil in my car (if I can find the dipstick) eludes me. When I buy something unassembled, my frustration level rises measurably as I fumble about trying to put it together.

How can I use my Practical Thinking strength more effectively in such a situation? One way is to read the directions carefully. The only problem is that directions, I believe, are often written to confuse rather than inform. How am I to attach "y" to "x" if I do not know how the two go together?

My tendency as a theoretical thinker is to try to dream up a way of doing the assembling without really stopping to survey the situation. I first try one way, then another, with my anxiety steadily increasing. Then someone comes along, looks over the situation (analyzes the problem), and finds the solution either by reading the directions or by using his/her practical experience gained in previous attempts.

I have the same problem when I have misplaced a letter or a sheet of paper on which I have outlined a class session. I begin looking through the many piles of paper on my desk, book shelves, and other places. (At this point I really envy my more practical friends whose filing systems work. As another friend, also stronger theoretically, once said to me, "I'm a piler, not a filer.") As I search frantically through stacks of unfiled magazines mixed with letters and papers, my wife will often say, "Now sit down and think about where it could be." Sometimes this works!

On these occasions I am not using my Practical Thinking strength to solve my problem. I need to become better organized so that I can face the problem calmly and systematically.

Practical Thinking strength used creatively makes it possible for us to deal with real situations, to organize and plan, and to move ahead with a minimum loss of motion and energy.

Theoretical Thinking

What is Theoretical Thinking? The key words in identifying this strength are *ideas, theories, hypotheses, imagination, innovation.* Whereas Practical Thinking makes it possible for us to see reality, Theoretical Thinking provides the basis for *seeing possibilities.* These possibilities are not necessarily new: there are only a few real innovators. Most of us borrow our ideas from other people. Then we use these ideas to solve problems and are therefore creating new possibilities.

Theoretical Thinking is not confined to philosophy and scientific research, where its use is obvious. I used Theoretical Thinking in dealing with my car when it failed to start. I had a theory which the mechanic tested and discarded.

Or suppose a light bulb fails to light up in our favorite lamp. Our reaction is so automatic that we do not think of it as based on theory: we try a new bulb. Actually, however, it is a theory on which we act, and if the theory proves wrong and the lamp still does not light, we must self-consciously find another theory to solve the problem.

It should be clear that we all engage in Theoretical Thinking. The question is whether we use our Theoretical Thinking *strength* to the full. I have a friend who has his job so well organized that should someone by chance suggest a new way of doing something his response is almost invariably, "It'll never work!" He thereby cuts himself off from the possibility of finding a better way to do his job.

To be sure, there are some routines that do not need to be disturbed, but not many. There is almost always the possibility that there is a better way if we will "only put our mind to it." The better routine usually does not happen by chance; it grows out of the vision of a possibility, and this is the result of Theoretical Thinking.

A Working Example

JW, the practical thinker from Chapter 2 (page 28), went to a new job. As was his custom, he spent the first few weeks surveying the situation (doing Practical Thinking). It was much worse than he had been led to believe it was. His first temptation was to bemoan his fate and blame those who had sold him on taking the new position.

But he put his experience in the Bi/Polar System to work, and soon began to realize that there were possibilities in the situation that his practical mind did not fully grasp. So he turned to the same friends who had persuaded him to take the job. They became defensive, tried to assure him that things were not as bad as he thought, and turned to more pleasant topics of conversation.

JW began to see that essentially he was on his own, and he spent long hours moving beyond his analysis of the situation to imagining possibilities. He drew upon past experiences and insights as well as printed resources, and began to see ways in which he could act creatively in the situation that at first had seemed hopeless. He then moved into action to plan and put his ideas to work. After a year on the job, the situation was turned around and others have begun to applaud him for his dynamic leadership.

JW deliberately *used* his Theoretical Thinking strength, and this was not easy for him since his greater Thinking strength is Practical. He did not fantasize by thinking of an ideal situation and wishing he were there, and there is a decisive difference in Theoretical Thinking and fantasy. Knowing that he needed help, he turned to the resources in his experience as well as printed ones to feed his imagination. He used his Risking strength to propel him toward a more creative use of Thinking. Without this kind of deliberate use of his strengths, he might have followed the path of least resistance and looked for another position.

Polarized on the Practical

When we *fail* to use both Practical Thinking and Theoretical Thinking strengths, we become polarized on one or the other. "Polarized" is the opposite of Bi/Polar, and means that we use one strength without the other. JW could easily have become polarized on his problems and never moved beyond them.

This was the case of a class I taught a few years ago. All members were pastors of small churches struggling to survive. Regardless of what I said, they always came back to their problems. "That won't work" was their repeated response to what I said or what they read. I finally became so angry that I told the men I was sick and tired of hearing about their problems and wanted them to move on to try to solve those problems. For the remainder of that class period we actually discussed possible solutions, but by the next day they were back on their problems. I was never able to move them off dead center to any kind of creative facing of their situations. They were polarized on the practical (their problems), and they tended toward a feeling of despair.

Or consider another kind of situation where it is easy to become polarized on the practical, that of the homemaker. Confronted by cleaning to be done, meals to be cooked, clothes to be washed and mended, and children to transport from one place to another, is it any wonder that some homemakers give way to boredom and others begin to work outside the home just to escape the routine? Another solution to their problem is to use Theoretical Thinking strength for two purposes: to think of better ways to carry out the routine, and of ways to relieve the boredom of the routine. For some the latter may consist of inviting a neighbor in for coffee; for others it will be taking time to read; for still others it will be developing creativity through some form of expressive activity.

This approach does not occur by chance. Rather, it requires imaginative planning of necessary work and of relief from such work through refreshing diversions. In other words, it requires the deliberate use of Theoretical Thinking strength.

Polarized on the Theoretical

We can also become polarized on the theoretical. This often happens to me. I frequently imagine I can do more than is realistic—and then waste time worrying because I have not done all I thought I could do. My only solution is to make a list, check things off the list as I do them, and have the satisfaction of knowing that I have moved ahead at the end of the day. It does not matter greatly that several items must usually be carried over until the next day. I have the satisfaction of working out a plan through using my Practical Thinking strength and following it. I even find that when I make such a list I am more realistic about what I can do and also work harder to accomplish what I have on my list.

Alice is a highly motivated, quite capable person. She does not have to work but would like the satisfaction of professional accomplishment. When she assumes a new position, she is highly enthusiastic about it but she seldom works at the same job for more than a few months. The problematical aspects of the position soon outweigh its advantages and she quickly loses her enthu-

siasm. So she goes on looking for the ideal job, polarized on the theoretical and unwilling to face the reality that almost no one finds all aspects of a particular job to his liking. Because of this she does not have the satisfaction of professional achievement, and many agencies that she could serve to their benefit are deprived of her skills.

A Blending of the Two

Thinking *can* become polarized on either the Practical or the Theoretical pole, but it need not be so. One of the purposes of this book is to help you learn how to use both aspects of your Thinking strength so that your thinking will be more creative. This joining of the two in creative interaction is what we called Bi/Polar Thinking in Chapter 2.

The use of Practical Thinking strength leads to a perception of reality. That is, it makes it possible for us to understand a situation or problem we face. Its contribution is to make it possible for us to see and understand *things as they are.*

The use of Theoretical Thinking strength leads to a perception of possibilities. That is, we can find a way of dealing with a situation and solving its problems. It enables us to see and understand *things as they might become.*

Bi/Polar Thinking is a blending of the two or the use of both Practical and Theoretical Thinking strengths in all aspects of life. The result is creative perception—the seeing of both reality and the possibilities of dealing with reality. It makes us aware of both the problems and possible solutions to them. As we move back and forth between the two, we are enabled to negotiate life with a maximum understanding of what confronts us and how we can cope with it. We cannot cope constructively except as we are both realistic about the limitations of life and the possibility of living creatively within its boundaries.

Making a Decision

The second decision you are asked to make in your journey toward deeper self-understanding is whether you are stronger in Practical or Theoretical Thinking. As an aid in this process, the following contrasts between persons should be helpful.

1. Persons higher in Practical Thinking are usually "down to earth" people, interested in practical, everyday things. Those higher in Theoretical Thinking are more likely to be dreamers, or at least interested in what might develop.

2. Those who lead with Practical Thinking often have a high level of tolerance for routine, and may resist changes in their personal lives. Those who lead with Theoretical Thinking are more likely to chafe under routine and to like, even look for, change.

3. Persons with greater Practical Thinking strength like to deal with real situations and with facts and data, and may be more aware of problems than solutions. Those with greater Theoretical Thinking strength enjoy theories, finding solutions to problems, seeing possibilities and potentialities.

4. Persons higher in Practical Thinking usually deal with situations realistically and may lack imagination. They go about their work with a concern for practical results. Those higher in Theoretical Thinking usually have more imagination, may be innovative, and are less interested in the immediate outcome of their work and better able to see the long-range possibilities of their lives.

Here are five key questions to answer as you seek to move toward greater self-understanding. Read them and make an "a" or "b" choice quickly. In instances where you do not find a clear decision easy, ask yourself which you are more inclined to be or to do.

1. Which do you enjoy most: (a) dealing with the real world _____ or (b) dealing with the world of ideas and possibilities _____?
2. Do you like to (a) dig in and get the facts _____ or (b) dream of possibilities, even daydream _____?
3. Are you better at understanding (a) facts and data _____ or (b) theories and ideas _____?
4. Which do you do better and more easily: (a) identify the problem _____ or (b) think up possible solutions to a problem _____?
5. When you do something a second time, do you (a) usually want to do it the same way you did it the first time _____ or (b) often want to make changes in the way you do it the second time _____?

If the "a's" clearly outnumber the "b's," you see yourself as stronger in Practical Thinking. If the "b's" clearly outnumber the "a's," you see yourself as higher in Theoretical Thinking. In case the results are indecisive, think about how you would like to spend your time if you were completely free. Do you think of practical, down-to-earth things? Or do you dream of being able to do things that are beyond your reach just now? This kind of thought process may help you in making your choice between the two kinds of Thinking.

You may have trouble in making a decision. One of the reasons is that the circumstances of life can thrust us into roles not altogether to our liking, and we become so accustomed to these roles that we do not know who we really are.

For example, people have been telling me all my life that I should be more practical—not always in words but sometimes in the ways in which I am rewarded. As a teacher it would appear that it would have been otherwise for me, for teaching involves the use of ideas. But the rewards of teaching do not come alone from the mastery of ideas; they also involve how one organizes and presents those ideas. The results of teaching can be seen best in the way students respond to a class. This is especially the case in a society where there are so many media to compete with: an abundance of well-written books, mass communication, and the like. I know this to be true because some of the teachers I have had who knew the most were among the least effective teachers.

It has therefore been difficult for me to accept the fact that I am more theoretical than practical. But when I begin to think about what I would most enjoy doing in life, I see a vision of a library, a desk, and a writing pad—and I know then that my *natural* inclination is toward the theoretical.

It may be this way with you—so try to get beneath the mask which you have been forced to wear, in order to decide who you really are. You may not be able to change the circumstances of your life, but you can act more creatively in relation to them when you know your real self.

Discussion and Activity Guide

1. List four differences in Practical and Theoretical Thinking strengths. With which list do you identify most readily?

2. Go back through the five statements with "a" and "b" choices. Make at least a tentative decision concerning where your greater strength lies in Practical or Theoretical Thinking. The key to your answer lies in whether your natural preference is in dealing with a real situation involving facts, data, and the identification of problems (Practical Thinking) or in dealing with ideas, theories, possibilities, and dreams (Theoretical Thinking).

3. Write your choice on your work sheet.

4. How would your life be different if you were able more often to follow your natural preference in these two strengths?

5. What can you do now to make your thinking more creative, as a blend of Practical and Theoretical Thinking?

–4–

Dependent and Independent Risking Strength

A five-year-old boy is having his evening meal. During a period of half an hour two adults have given him various instructions including several "No's." "No, you can't eat right this minute; dinner isn't ready." "Wash your hands." ("But I did.") "Well, do it again." "Eat your chicken." "No, you can't put sugar and soy sauce both on your rice." "Don't you want to drink your milk?"

Finally the child says with a note of desperation, "Leave me alone!" The adults recognize that he has reached a breaking point, and they leave him completely out of their conversation for the next few minutes. Soon, to attract their attention, he is crawling under the table. He is unwilling to be ignored and desires to be back in a relationship with them even though five minutes earlier he had demanded that he be allowed to be by himself.

This simple incident illustrates two of the deepest emotional needs of human beings. These are the need *to be in relationship* with others and the need *to be apart* from them. That is, we need to be loved and to be secure, but we also need to be allowed freedom to be and to become ourselves.

For the affiliative needs (love, security) Gordon Allport

used the picturesque term *tribalism*. *Individuation* was the term he chose to denote the need for autonomy (freedom, the right to be and become). Beginning in infancy, these emotional impulses persist into adulthood. As Allport put it, throughout life each person "will be attempting to reconcile these two modes of becoming, the tribal and the personal [individuation]: the one that makes him into a mirror, the other that lights the lamp of individuality within." [1]

In a real sense what I will be doing in this chapter is an expansion of this statement from one of the leading twentieth-century humanistic psychologists. I am using the Bi/Polar System as the source for three seldom recognized insights concerning these generally accepted human qualities—the need to belong and the need to be apart.

First, we will look at them not just as personal *attributes* but as *strengths*. The two strengths are Dependent Risking and Independent Risking.

Second, the chapter will help you identify which of these is stronger in your God-given make-up. It is at this point that the Bi/Polar System makes a unique contribution to self-understanding. While agreeing with most psychological systems that the two are present in every human being, it makes the further assertion that one is always stronger than the other. An important step in your self-understanding is the decision concerning which of these strengths—Dependent or Independent Risking—is stronger in your individuality.

Third, we will provide in this chapter the first step in your seeing how the two can work together to produce more creative living. Bi/Polar Risking, which we considered in Chapter 2, is a blend of the two in creative interaction. Both are necessary for creative living, and neither is more valuable than the other in the life process.

---

[1] Gordon W. Allport, *Becoming: Basic Consideration for a Psychology of Personality* (New Haven: Yale University Press, 1955), p. 35.

Dependent Risking

What do we mean by Dependent Risking? The strength of Dependent Risking is based on the human need to belong, to be loved, to have a reasonable degree of security. Those stronger in Dependent Risking tend to be *other-*directed. Their natural tendency is both *to draw strength from others* and *to offer strength* to them. They make good group members, work well as part of a team, listen to others, take advice. They are naturally cooperative and usually enjoy a wide range of relationships.

CW is an administrator in an academic setting. He is efficient in his work, which involves details, because of his strong Practical Thinking. But his greatest strength is Dependent Risking, and his life revolves around people. He remembers names easily, is constantly on call to listen to students, has a steady stream of people spending time in his home. Everyone likes him, and he is the center of an informal noon group that regularly bring their lunches to eat in his office. He is the reconciler in groups, with the ability to bring harmony between those who disagree.

DL is a Theoretical Thinker but also highly relational. She is witty, charming, able to bring life and vivacity to others. When the routine of one job becomes distasteful, she simply goes out and finds another. She has served with ease as both mother and father to her elementary-age child.

ME is stronger in Bi/Polar Thinking than Bi/Polar Risking, more Dependent than Independent. Her husband is a clergyman. When he was appointed to a new church, she found the women's group divided between an older, entrenched group and one composed of younger women. She began to think and develop a way of dealing with the situation. Able to relate well to the younger group, she maintained a good relationship with the older one also. One part of her strategy was to ask the leaders of the older group for help on every possible occasion. In this way she has been able to help the younger group feel more of a sense of ownership for the group without antagonizing the older one.

RM was a young college student who died of cancer at age twenty-one. He had been taken into the home of an older couple when he was in his teens, and he brought life and vitality to their lives. Always desiring to please others, he adapted easily to the life style of his foster parents and began to take on many of the colorations of their progressive stand on such issues as integration. After his death, one young woman whom his foster parents did not know wrote: "I want you to know that R. spent many hours listening to and helping me with my problems. . . . Even though I only met R. a few times, his loving concern helped me through many hard times . . . R. was so nice to me—almost a complete stranger. I hope that I can be as helpful to others as he was to me." A couple wrote to say simply, "R. brought a lot of joy into our lives and we'll miss him." A more mature woman from his college wrote that he frequently dropped by her office "to brighten our day with reports of the progress he was making in his classes and to share little moments of his life." A young woman who had been a good friend for six years wrote: "He has given me so much joy and love it is hard to explain, but I know you understand." And his foster parents did, for he had done the same thing for them.

The great gift to life of those high in Dependent Risking strength is the ability to do what the letters quoted in the last case indicate: to bring joy and reconciliation to others.

Those high in Dependent Risking strength both *depend on others* and allow *others to draw strength* from them. Others can *learn* to do the same; those high in Dependent Risking are *naturally* endowed with a great degree of this gift.

Independent Risking

What is Independent Risking? This strength is based on the natural inclination *to depend on one's self,* or to be autonomous. Persons higher in Independent Risking often *stand alone* as they follow their convictions. They almost always have great *self-respect, self-confidence,* and *self-esteem.* Often preferring to work independently, they cause things to happen. They are the ones who naturally move things forward—the dynamic company president, the forceful preacher, the leader of those who willingly follow. Others can *learn* these skills; Independent Riskers *naturally* behave in these ways.

RT came to an academic situation from a successful career in the local church to begin a new program of continuing education. A colleague had been considering an idea for a special training program for local church educators who had not attended theological school. Either because he could not or would not, he had taken no action to implement the idea. He presented it to RT whose immediate response was, "Let's do it." The program was launched in a few months and has continued since that time.

Linda was a secretary when she attended a Bi/Polar Seminar, working so that her husband could give full time to his studies. "I'm bored to death with my work," she reported to the Bi/Polar instructor. He encouraged her to find an outlet for her strong Independent Risking strength and advised her husband to help make this possible if he wanted their marriage to endure. Linda soon quit her full-time job and enrolled in a course in interior design. This work provided her with an outlet for her dynamic personality and freed her from the routines involved in secretarial work for which she was not suited.

JMB has made her way in a "man's world" (prior to the feminist movement) by using her Independent Risking strength for professional competency and as an aid in helping her relate effectively to the all-male world in which she has moved. Early in her professional career she determined that she would find ways by which she could help her male colleagues achieve their goals and at the same time achieve hers. In one instance she served as a member of a politically elected board most of whose members acted out of concerns almost diametrically opposite to hers. Through her practical wisdom, she chose the battles she thought she might be able to win and did not push those she knew she could not. By deliberately relating to the other members of the board in terms of their needs, she was able to secure their cooperation and advance the causes she chose to espouse with the other board members.

J. W. Thomas is an Independent Thinker. His innovative mind, as we have seen, produced the ideas on which this book is based. His Independent Risking has been expressed through his careful thinking and his persistence even when opposition arose. He has stood by his convictions even when questions have arisen, and he has refused to allow the basic design of his innovative system of thought to be corrupted.

The great gift of those stronger in Independent Risking strength is to provide dynamic leadership either in action or in thinking. They make things happen, take a stand,

and stay by their convictions. They begin new enterprises, think new thoughts, provide leadership, and become those to whom others turn (charismatic leaders, they are sometimes called).

Polarized on Dependent Risking

Although we are stronger in one of these strengths than in the other, we have both and must use both in interaction. When we fail to use both, we become polarized on (or overuse) one strength at the expense of the other.

To be polarized on Dependent Risking means to become overly-dependent *on* others or to allow others to become overly-dependent *on us*. This is one of the reasons that dependence is sometimes interpreted as a weakness. (The other reason is that our culture tends to place greater value on independence than on dependence.) Actually Dependent Risking *is* a strength, but like all strengths it can be overused and even misused.

LW is a highly relational person who expresses her Dependent Risking more fully by making others dependent on her. She is married to an Independent Thinker who enjoys being alone, a fact which LW has found it difficult to understand. After she had been through a Bi/Polar Seminar, she began to see how she had been polarized on Dependent Risking. For the first time she understood why her husband did not want as close a relationship to her and others as she desired. "I've learned," she said, "to let Roy go in the den and close the door and be by himself. Then I call up a friend and talk on the telephone for an hour."

DL, the charming, winsome, young woman previously described (page 48), tends to misuse her Dependent Risking strength by becoming overly-dependent on others. This is exacerbated by the fact that her life has brought responsibilities far beyond those with which most persons her age must cope. Her tendency is to let others take over her life, though she is struggling against this tendency toward polarization. An older friend, whose dependency needs are expressed primarily in the desire for others to depend on him, has made it far too easy for her to rely on him. Both are striving to lessen the dependency relationship that they now recognize as not being healthy for either.

A more common way in which those high in Dependent Risking become polarized is to allow others to "rule their lives." They may be afraid to express their opinions until others have done so lest they harm the relationship. They find it difficult to say "no" to those who make demands on their time. If this condition persists, they will lose their self-respect and eventually the respect of others also.

Dependent Risking is a strength; it can produce good relationships, the willingness to trust others, and the ability to be a reconciler of differences. Without those who exercise the strength, life would tend to become wholly competitive. It is Dependent Risking strength that makes human community possible. Like all strengths, however, Dependent Risking can be abused, overused, and misused.

Polarized on Independent Risking

Those higher in Independent Risking can also become polarized. One of their temptations is to believe that they can do things better than anyone else, and they therefore find it difficult to delegate responsibility. By their natural ability to provide leadership, they may also develop a love of power for its own sake. Their self-esteem can become conceit, and their self-confidence may lead them to become "pushy." They thus tend to cut themselves off from all except a small circle of dependent friends. When they misuse their strength in these ways, they eventually lose their own self-respect.

David is a strong Independent Risker, married to a women who is a Dependent Thinker. He had ruled her life, though he expected from her the same kind of dynamic leadership he himself was able to give. In a Bi/Polar Seminar, she began to express her independence more articulately. Much to his surprise, she told him in clear words that she felt suppressed and intimidated. His response was, "Why haven't you told me that before?"

William is an ambitious, independent businessman whose goal was to make his first million by the age of thirty-five. He was doing well in business until he entered into a business adventure with two partners who abandoned the enterprise when it began to falter. William was left with responsibility for a sizable debt. Since he was extremely conscientious, he refused to declare bankruptcy and sought ways to pay the debt. His independence made it distasteful for him to ask for help, and under the pressures he began to drink excessively. His self-esteem deteriorated and he felt himself to be a failure. It was only when he began to be willing to ask others for help that his self-esteem began to return and he was able to begin the process of dealing constructively with his problems.

TW is an Independent Thinker who is both innovative and creative. His temptation has not been to exercise power over others but to reject them and live in isolation with his ideas. "A very definite characteristic which I recognize clearly as I reflect about my past life is the tendency to cut people off entirely," he writes. "As far back as I can remember, when the occasion would arise in a relationship that caused me to experience emotional rejection of the person, I would do so with practically no personal pain. In fact, it was done with a good deal of self-confidence and self-satisfaction."

Women and Independent Risking

It has been difficult to find illustrations of women who have become polarized on Independent Risking. In a male-dominated culture, they have found it difficult to express their independence in business or the professions. In these enterprises they have usually been forced to temper their independence in order to adjust to the stereotype that a woman ought to help a man "look good" when the two are in competition. They have often been told, "Let a man win if you want him to marry you."

There are three ways in which, prior to the feminist movement, women have dealt with their Independent Risking strength outside the home. First, there have been a few professions in which they were allowed to be themselves. For example, my entire experience as an elementary student was in a school with a woman as principal, and I remember her as quite a dominant person. Second, they have also found ways in women's organizations, such as the Y.W.C.A., to exercise their leadership. One woman I know decided many years ago that there was no opportunity in the church for her as a woman to channel her concern for human welfare. Consequently, she turned to the Y.W.C.A. where she had once worked professionally and served for eighteen years with distinction on its national board.

A third way in which they have expressed their dynamic leadership is to blend it with their Dependent Risking. This bi/polar approach, though not derived from the Bi/Polar System, is essentially what the Bi/Polar System proposes. It consists of the deliberate use of both Dependent and Independent Risking strengths together. It leads to both good relationships with and confidence in others and confidence in one's self.

What I have described in the previous paragraph is what we mean by Bi/Polar Risking. The person higher in Dependent Risking begins with his/her dependence on others and uses it to gain more self-confidence. The person higher in Independent Risking risks him/her self in relation to others and, therefore, grows in relationships.

For example, a friend of mine, whose greater Risking strength is Independence, has learned that he must delegate authority if his work is to be completed. He must often work with his assistant until the appropriate skill has been attained. As he delegates to others, he is able to do more himself, and he, therefore, grows in both self-confidence and confidence in others.

On the other hand, I must proceed in quite a different manner. I have always been afraid to submit my work to others, especially my writing. I have learned that I must use my Dependent Risking to ask help from others. When I do, my work improves and I grow both in self-confidence and in confidence in others. As my Independence Risking strength increases, I am better able both to accept and reject the advice I receive from others.

Making a Choice

The third decision you are asked to make in your movement toward greater self-understanding concerns your greater strength in Risking, either Dependent or Independent. The following contrasts between persons is offered as a way of moving you toward this decision.

1. Persons stronger in Dependent Risking like to be around people much, perhaps most, of the time. They often find it difficult to be alone. Those higher in Independent Risking are less interested in such relationships and often enjoy being alone.

2. Persons who lead with Dependent Risking usually prefer to work at a task in relation to others, especially in a group. Those who lead with Independent Risking usually prefer to work alone even though they may be forced by circumstances to work with a group. They may say, "If I could just do this myself, I could get it done better and more quickly."

3. Persons with greater Dependent Risking strength usually have confidence in others, and may lack self-confidence. Those with greater Independent Risking strength often lack confidence in others and almost always have considerable self-confidence.

4. Persons higher in Dependent Risking usually find it easy to listen to others and often difficult to follow their own convictions. Those higher in Independent Risking may find it difficult to listen to others and prefer to follow their own understanding of how things are or ought to be.

Here are five key questions to answer as you seek to determine where your greater strength lies. Read them and make an "a" or "b" choice quickly. In instances where you do not find a clear decision easy, ask yourself which you are more inclined to be or to do.

1. Are you (a) naturally cooperative _____ or (b) more individualistic _____?
2. Do you find it (a) relatively easy to take advice from others _____ or (b) easier to follow your own convictions _____?
3. Do you (a) sometimes have problems in having enough self-esteem _____ or (b) do you usually have fairly high self-esteem _____?
4. Do you (a) often feel the need to get the opinions of others _____ or (b) do you generally feel fairly self-sufficient _____?
5. Do you prefer (a) to work with a group _____ or (b) work by yourself _____?

If the "a's" clearly outnumber the "b's," you see yourself as stronger in Dependent Risking. If the "b's" clearly outnumber the "a's," you see yourself as stronger in Independent Risking. If the results are indecisive, consider what you would prefer to do or to be if you were entirely free. Reread the case studies in the chapter to see with which group you most readily identify. Try to get beneath the way life has forced you to behave and discover your real feelings. The basic question is: Does it come easier for you to depend on others and/or let others depend on you? Or to stand alone and enjoy your own achievements?

The Bi/Polar System

We have now concluded our survey of the Bi/Polar System of understanding people. It is deceptively simple. Three pairs of strengths do not seem like much with which to work, but they give us a surprisingly great amount of information about ourselves.

There are other components of personality, of course, and we will review some of these in a later chapter. Although none of these components alone *determine* who we are and who we become, they are all influential. One of the forces that we will later consider is personal choice. Choices are influenced by our value system and our faith, and they in turn make a great difference in what we do with our Bi/Polar strengths. How we *use* our strengths is a crucial question, the result of which is either creative or uncreative living.

Chart 1 is a simple visual summary of the Bi/Polar System. Creative living is the result of our choosing to use

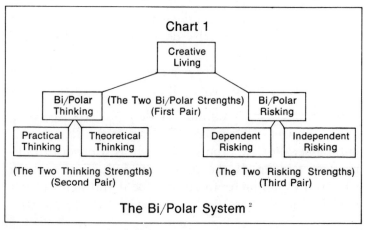

Chart 1

Creative Living

Bi/Polar Thinking   (The Two Bi/Polar Strengths)   Bi/Polar Risking
(First Pair)

Practical Thinking   Theoretical Thinking   Dependent Risking   Independent Risking

(The Two Thinking Strengths)   (The Two Risking Strengths)
(Second Pair)   (Third Pair)

The Bi/Polar System [2]

our strengths in relation to one another in the light of our central loyalty. This center of loyalty in the Jewish-Christian heritage is the Creator, the merciful God who seeks to bring his human children to their full potential. For the Christian, the center is God as known through Jesus Christ. Knowing and using our strengths creatively can be a tool for helping us in the struggle to live a centered life.

You have been asked to choose your greater strength in each of the three pairs of strengths. This does not mean, as I have repeatedly said, that you do not have strength in the polar opposites of your major strengths. It is a matter of where *your greater strength* lies in each pair.

All of the strengths are good, and it is good for you to be stronger in either one of each pair. For self-understanding and more creative living, you need to know what your greater strengths are. As you affirm yourself, you will become increasingly true to the self given to you in creation. When you learn to use the strengths in interaction with one another, you will be able to cope with life and move toward being the person God intends you to be.

Discussion and Activity Guide

1. List four characteristics of both Dependent and Independent Risking. With which list do you most readily identify?

2. Go back through the five statements with "a" and "b" choices. Make at least a tentative decision concerning where your greater strength lies in Dependent and Independent Risking.

3. Write your decision on your work sheet. You now have your three major strengths that form the pattern of your individuality. These patterns are discussed in Chapter 5.

4. What do you tend to do that is a result of your overuse or misuse of your greater strength in the polar pair of Dependent and Independent Risking?

5. What do you need to do to work out a better blend of Dependent and Independent Risking?

6. Review the chart on page 58 as an overview of the Bi/Polar System of understanding people.

The *eight patterns of strengths* are described in this chapter. If you have already decided on your major strength in each of the pairs, you may want to read this chapter in segments. After reading the introduction, go directly to the pattern which your selection of major strengths fits. If you have not made this decision, then read until you find a pattern with which you feel comfortable. Eventually you will need to read the material concerning all the patterns to help you in understanding other people.

The major strengths in the eight patterns are:

Pattern One: Bi/Polar Thinking, Practical Thinking, Dependent Risking

Pattern Two: Bi/Polar Thinking, Practical Thinking, Independent Risking

Pattern Three: Bi/Polar Thinking, Theoretical Thinking, Dependent Risking

Pattern Four: Bi/Polar Thinking, Theoretical Thinking, Independent Risking

Pattern Five: Bi/Polar Risking, Dependent Risking, Practical Thinking

Pattern Six: Bi/Polar Risking, Dependent Risking, Theoretical Thinking

Pattern Seven: Bi/Polar Risking, Independent Risking, Practical Thinking

Pattern Eight: Bi/Polar Risking, Independent Risking, Theoretical Thinking

After you have tried out one or more patterns and have come to some decision, however tentative, about yourself, then read the concluding part of the chapter on pattern blends.

–5–

Your Patterns of Strengths

Throughout my life I have wanted to be more dynamic. I am ambitious, and I observed that dynamic people were more often given positions of leadership and received more recognition. I was also conditioned by my culture to believe that people could be anything they set out to be. I read—"devoured" might be a better word—the Horatio Alger books when I was young, and in those books the hero always became the company president or achieved some comparable goal.

I tried, and sometimes I succeeded, though often the harder I tried the more anxious and guilty I felt. I found it easy to excel in school, and I remained a student as long as possible. Then when I could no longer justify playing the student role, I became a teacher. But I found that in academic circles it is the administrators who both receive greater recognition and higher salaries, and my problem continued.

I went on doing my work—teaching and writing—but I seldom felt really good about myself. I kept on wanting to be someone whom God did not create me to be—that kind of leader who in academic circles is asked to be a dean, or at least an associate dean.

As I now look back on my life, I realize that I was rebelling against God in my unwillingness to accept thankfully the gifts he had given me in creation, and use them without complaining that I did not have other strengths. My problem did not grow out of a lack of faith; rather, it was the result of a lack of self-understanding and self-acceptance.

The identification of my greater strengths through the use of the Bi/Polar System was a freeing experience for me. I came to see—and accept—that I am stronger in Bi/Polar Thinking, Theoretical Thinking, and Dependent Risking. I suppose that if I had been placed in an administrative position I could have muddled through, but I realize now that I would have been miserable in trying to do so.

Your response to this personal confession may be, "So what? Most people don't achieve all they want to in life. What's new?" Or you may be thinking, "That's par for the course. What can I do about it?"

Patterns of Strengths

The answer to these questions is what this chapter is all about. It is concerned with *patterns of strengths* and *what they mean*. It is designed to help you see how you naturally react to and act upon life's circumstances when you have a particular combination of strengths. These patterns help identify the "set" of your personality. They are the beginning point for *the use of all your strengths* in becoming a more adequate person.

These *common* characteristics of people must be seen in relation to the fact that *no two people are exactly alike*. We sometimes say when we refer to an unusual person, "When God made Joe, he threw away the pattern." Well, that is true of everyone.

There are many components in personality. The amount of native intelligence we have is important, as is our energy level. Even our physical endowment and our health help to make us who we are. Our present stage of development —factors identified by developmental theorists—is crucial. A child does not think in the same way an adult does, for example.

Outside forces are also important—our environment in the past and the present. Children who are not talked and read to by adults in their young years may be permanently impaired in their verbal skills. The lack of love—in the touch and tone of the voice of significant adults in a child's life—may leave scars throughout life. Cultural anthropologists have provided important data that point to the fact that personality is formed by the interaction of an individual with his/her environment, especially the significant adults in the life of the child.

But there are also ways in which we are all alike. I pointed out two of these ways in Chapter 4—the need to be loved and the need to be free. Psychologists who have studied human growth and development—Jean Piaget and Erik Erikson to name only two—help us understand *stages* of human development that are the same in all people. Gail Sheehy in her best-selling book *Passages* [3] has extended this kind of study into adulthood by identifying what she believes are "predictable crises of adult life."

Our approach to these common characteristics of people is not developmental, however. The Bi/Polar System identifies eight *patterns of strengths* that help us understand who we are. Some people have problems in identifying their pattern because life has forced them to be someone they were not born to be. Others have learned to use their strengths so creatively that they have almost forgotten who they naturally are. I cannot *guarantee* that you will be able to decide which pattern fits you best. I can assure you that if you will stay with this book to the end, you have a good chance of doing so.

---

[3] Gail Sheehy, *Passages: Predictable Crises of Adult Life* (New York: E. P. Dutton & Co., Inc., 1974, 1976).

CHART 2
THE BI/POLAR SYMBOL

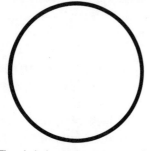

The circle is used to represent the bounds of the personality.

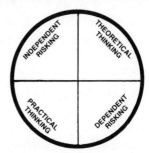

The four quadrants of the circle each represent a single strength, with the two opposite quadrants composing the Bi/Polar strength.

The axis from bottom left to top right represents Bi/Polar Thinking.

The axis from bottom right to top left represents Bi/Polar Risking.

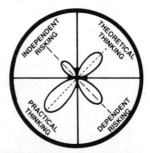

The loops extending along the axes represent the relative strengths for a particular pattern. This figure is the symbol for Pattern One.

CHART 3

EIGHT PATTERNS OF POLAR STRENGTHS

1

REALISTIC
(real world)

2

Stable
Dependable
People-oriented
Loose ship
Warm
Maintains
  Stability

TYPICAL PROBLEMS:
Needs more
  self-confidence
Underrates self

Objective
Independent
Task-oriented
Tight ship
Efficient
Reserved
Initiates stability

TYPICAL PROBLEMS:
Trusting others
Over critical of others

3

IDEALISTIC
(ideas)

4

Theoretical
Cooperative
Philosophical
Considerate
Cultured
Academic

TYPICAL PROBLEMS:
Needs more
  self-confidence
Exaggerates
  own weakness

Inventive
Independent
Individualistic
Insightful
Reserved
Loner

TYPICAL PROBLEMS:
Depending on others
Dealing with reality

5

WARM
(other people)

6

Outgoing
Practical
Aggresively helpful
Sociable
Coordinator
Trusts others

TYPICAL PROBLEMS:
Says "Yes" when
  should say "No"
Needs more
  self-confidence

Outgoing
Intuitive "feel"
Diplomatic
Romantic
Idealistic
Emotionally
  expressive

TYPICAL PROBLEMS:
Idealizes people
Lets others run their life

7

ASSERTIVE
(self)

8

Self-starter
Enterprising
Self-confident
Forceful
Competitive
Hard driver
Initiator

TYPICAL PROBLEMS:
Impatience
Talks when should
  be listening

Dynamic
Persuasive
Optimistic
Promotor
Sells a dream
Stimulates
  change

TYPICAL PROBLEMS:
Talks when
  should be listening
Fails to see problems

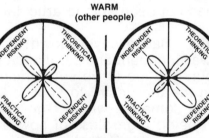

J. W. Thomas, *Bi/Polar: A Positive Way of Understanding People* (Richardson, Texas:
BI/POLAR, Incorporated, 1978), p. 54. Used by permission.

Are Patterns Limiting?

Perhaps by now you are thinking what people sometimes say in our Bi/Polar seminars: "I don't want to be limited by a pattern. I just want to use all my strengths and be what I want to be." Others are less polite and use words to this effect: "Don't box me in—I want to be free."

The personality patterns of this chapter are not meant to box you in. Rather, they are intended to provide you a base from which you can operate more effectively in coping with life. They help you know how *you, with your particular pattern of strengths, can learn to use all of them more creatively.*

One person said it this way:

I don't feel that the Bi/Polar System puts me in a box. In fact it has had the opposite effect on me. Because I understand my major strengths more fully, I find that I have been freed to express all my strengths in a way that I had been "feeling for" but had not been able to articulate or implement.

Basically, I had always known that my least strength was independence, but because my culture encouraged me to be enterprising and had instilled in me the desire to succeed, I kept on trying to be someone whom I never quite succeeded in being regardless of how hard I tried. Now I know that my greatest strength is Thinking, and I can be less anxious when I do not make the "big splash" or receive the recognition that some people do.

If I'm in a box at all, it's certainly an open-ended one. It provides me with a place where I can put my feet but from which I am freed to range widely, anchored in a recognition of my true self. As a matter of fact, I think I had previously been in a box without knowing it. Now, the recognition and acceptance of my natural en-

dowment has freed me to move more freely outside the box in the security that my greater
self-esteem provides for me.

Although there are predictable ways in which persons
with a particular pattern of strengths usually face life,
these ways can be modified. The eight patterns which we
will describe soon provide what Christian psychologist
Wayne Oates some years ago called the "stack-pole of personality." A stack-pole is an upright pole around which a
haystack is formed. This center pole holds the haystack
together, but the shape of the stack is the result of how
the hay is piled around it.

The way in which personality evolves, as we have seen,
is the result of many forces. One of these is the stack-pole
—those qualities which come to us as a gift of creation.
But the personality is shaped as this core interacts with
other factors, including our commitment and faith.

I hope by now you are convinced that I am not trying to
put you in a box. Rather, I am concerned that you learn,
in terms of your own pattern of strengths, to use all you
are to become the person God intended you to be. Your
pattern of strengths provides a launching pad from which
you can soar into orbit!

Remember also that this book is a tool, not a blueprint,
for helping you in this process. If you begin to use the pattern numbers as if they were molds into which people are
to be poured, then I have not been careful enough in my
explanation. Although the pattern descriptions which follow provide ways of talking about people with common
characteristics, no two people are exactly alike. However,
knowing our pattern of strengths can be of inestimable
service in learning to cope with life and to be more creative in our approach to life.

As a reminder of what we have already discussed in
Chapters 2, 3, and 4, I want to summarize briefly the data
on which the patterns of strengths are based.

1. *The first pair of strengths consists of Bi/Polar Thinking and Bi/Polar Risking.* You have both of these strengths, but

If you are stronger in Bi/Polar Thinking, you tend to think rather than feel your way through life. You usually make decisions deliberately on the basis of thinking. You probably enjoy planning more than doing, are more cautious than adventuresome, and think before you speak.

If you are stronger in Bi/Polar Risking, you tend to feel rather than think your way through life, sometimes or often acting on impulse rather than careful thought. You are probably more interested in people—yourself or others —than in ideas or facts. In all likelihood you are adventuresome in one or more areas of your life.

2. *The second pair of strengths consists of the two kinds of Thinking—Practical and Theoretical.* You have both of these strengths, but

If you are stronger in Practical Thinking, you tend to be factual, down-to-earth, concerned more with facts than with ideas. You are probably realistic about life and tend to accept things as they are until you are given a good reason for changing them. You ask "How?" questions.

If you are stronger in Theoretical Thinking, you usually enjoy new ideas; you tend to ask "Why?"; and you may be impatient with those who are not interested in theories. You may be tempted to dream about what might be rather than facing realistically what is.

3. *The third pair of strengths consists of Dependent Risking and Independent Risking.* You have both of these strengths, but

If your greater strength is Dependent Risking, you will be people-oriented to some degree, perhaps quite strongly. You may be either more inclined to let others depend on you, or depend on others, or both. Your tendency is to seek the help of others especially in areas of your life where you lack self-confidence.

If your greater strength is Independent Risking, you will

usually be self-confident, and you may feel that you can do things better than others. It will often be difficult for you to delegate authority, especially in those areas of your life that you consider most important. You will often have strong opinions, and you may enjoy your power either in thinking or acting, over situations or over people.

If you have problems in deciding where your greater strength lies in any of the three polar pairs, go back to the chapter that pertains to that pair and read it again.

The Eight Patterns of Strengths

Each pattern of strengths has a major strength in each of the three polar pairs. When you have decided on your three major strengths, you are ready to move directly to the pattern that includes those three. If you have not come to this conclusion, you will need to browse through all the patterns for additional help in making the decision.

Patterns One through Four have Bi/Polar Thinking in common, and Patterns Five through Eight, Bi/Polar Risking. Patterns One, Two, Five, and Seven are stronger in Practical Thinking, the other four in Theoretical Thinking. Patterns One, Three, Five, and Six lead with Dependent Risking, the other four with Independent Risking.

As a further means of determining your pattern, select the descriptive words under a pattern that seems to fit. You should be able to find a pattern where you can underline eighteen to twenty of the words or phrases listed. An additional aid is the reading of the case studies. Ask yourself with which of these persons you identify most readily.

PATTERN ONE—STABLE AND DEPENDABLE

Major strengths are: *Bi/Polar Thinking, Practical Thinking,* and *Dependent Risking.* The least strength is Independent Risking.

Typical characteristics are: [4] Ones tend to be consistent, cooperative, kind, factual, considerate, good listeners, organized, thoughtful, steady, dependable, quiet, practical, cautious; to hide their feelings; to be orderly, deliberate, gentle, stable; to have a "live and let live" attitude; to be team players; to run a "loose ship"; to be agreeable; to like people; to be concerned for others, down-to-earth, accepting, likeable; to have their "feet on the ground," to accept advice, to maintain the status quo.

Mary C. is a private secretary in her 40s with a stronger-than-average relational quality to her Practical Thinking. She is efficient in her work, loyal to her employer, and maintains an orderly though somewhat cluttered office. Her work sometimes suffers because she allows friends to impose upon her time as she listens to their problems. Nevertheless, she is careful not to let them interfere with the eventual completion of her work. She admits to thinking negatively about herself, and has learned to relate to her assertive husband by maintaining her own personal world. Instead of asking for help from others in her work, for fear of imposing on them and displeasing her employer, she often works overtime but feels like a martyr in doing so.

JW (see pages 28 and 39) is a clergyman who has developed a greater capacity to use both his Theoretical Thinking and Independent Risking than most Pattern Ones. As a consequence he often seems more dynamic than his natural inclination is to be. He is clear, however, that he prefers to draw ideas and encouragement from others when they are willing to provide them. He is able to take the ideas of others and organize

---

[4] The words and phrases used to describe each pattern are from *Bi/Polar: A Positive Way of Understanding People*, by J. W. Thomas (Richardson, Texas: BI/POLAR, Incorporated, 1978), and are used by permission.

them into workable plans. Although he deals fairly successfully with his temptation toward low self-esteem, it is still a struggle for him. His preferred way of working is to go into a new situation, analyze it carefully, draw ideas from others, and then go quietly about his work of bringing order and stability into the situation. His natural inclination is to listen to others, but he talks readily and enthusiastically when he has confidence in his ability to deal with the subject under discussion.

RT is an administrator in an academic situation who has developed the program for which he is responsible in a sound and expansive manner. In doing so, he has drawn considerably on the dynamic president of the college, on an associate who is highly relational, and on an assistant who is a better organizer than he is. Although he has been quite successful in his job, he confesses to still having negative thoughts about himself. He is thorough and well-organized in his public presentations, but he is not exciting. One gets the impression that his success in his work derives from deliberate and faithful attention to following through on details, based on a stable, dependable plan which draws upon the strengths of others for its implementation.

JL is an office manager whose relationship strength is seen more clearly in her personal relationships than in her business practices. Orderly, efficient, almost overly concerned with details, she neither neglects them nor allows others to do so. She brings order into a small business enterprise, and seldom allows even the most trivial matter to be neglected. Quiet in the presence of business associates, she speaks only to bring order out of their tendency to neglect details. But she can be vivacious and fun in social situations where she feels secure and at home.

President Dwight D. Eisenhower exemplifies
the characteristics of Pattern One. During World
War II, he was responsible for overall planning
and for trying to bring the competitive allies together, for dealing with tactical generals whose
egocentricity sometimes made them seem more
like rivals than allies, and for keeping the entire
operation mobile. He appointed aggressive leaders such as General George Patton to plan and
carry through battle operations, but after the war
found it necessary to place less aggressive leaders in charge.

Considered at first as a possible Democratic
candidate for President, he was the Republican
candidate in 1952 and won in spite of the fact
that he had, as William Manchester puts it, no
politics and "few known views on most of the
great issues of the times." [5] "His concept of leadership," as Manchester describes it, "reflected
his faith in experts and the delegation of authority." [6] He depended both in war and peace on
more flamboyant leaders, such as General Patton
and John Foster Dulles, his Secretary of State.
As President he maintained a low-key image and
was probably more of a father figure than a dynamic leader.

In all of these people, we see such characteristics as
stability, dependability, organizing ability, and the willingness to use the strengths of others to complement their
own. In most there is a tendency to have low self-confidence and often to think negatively about their own abilities. They earn the respect of others by a faithful execution
of their responsibilities rather than by a naturally scintillating personality.

[5] William Manchester, *The Glory and the Dream: A Narrative
History of America 1932–1972* (Boston: Little, Brown and Company, 1973, 1974), Volume One, p. 745.
[6] *Ibid.*, p. 791.

PATTERN TWO—REALISTIC AND INDEPENDENT

Major strengths are: *Bi/Polar Thinking, Practical Thinking,* and *Independent Risking.* The least strength is Dependent Risking.

Typical characteristics are: they tend to be objective; to have their "feet on the ground"; to be individualistic, reserved, realistic, disciplinarian, self-sufficient, competitive, practical, ambitious; to maintain control; to have a "bulldog tenacity"; to be loners; to "run a tight ship"; to be stable leaders, efficient, uncompromising; to represent the establishment; to be consistent, blunt, observant, serious, stoic, strong-willed, analytical, critical; to hold their feelings within; to be factual; to maintain law and order; to follow their own convictions.

RC is a business man who has carried out his responsibilities efficiently, successfully, and in a controlled manner. He is taciturn almost to the point of seeming unfriendly. This failure to speak up has resulted in his not advancing in the firm of which he is a part as far as his abilities warrant. In a Bi/Polar Seminar, he began to see the need of more openness to others and carefully planned a proposal to make to his associates. To his surprise, they not only listened but accepted the proposal that he had formulated with great care.

In his personal relationships he manifests the same quiet and reserved stance. He is married to an outgoing woman who has had problems in accepting his lack of closeness. In spite of this attitude, one gets the impression that he is still in control, however, able to maintain stability in what would otherwise be a free-flowing family situation. This control includes himself, and one can only wonder what is going on inside this highly disciplined person.

AW is an unusually stable, disciplined thinker who acts on his own convictions regardless of the consequences. At one time his associates never knew what he was thinking when he was in a group. When a decision was made with which he disagreed, he often gave way to his temptation not to voice his opinion and later to ignore as much as possible whatever decision had been made. As a result of insights received through the Bi/Polar inventory of his strengths, he became freer in expressing his convictions, though always in a controlled and laconic manner. As he did so, his relationships with his colleagues improved and they grew not only in their respect but also in their appreciation of him as a person.

He is married to a dynamic, independent woman. As their relationship has matured, they have been able to grant freedom to one another that allows each to assert his/her independence in creative ways. Some people find it difficult to understand, but those who know them well realize that there is both respect and deep affection between them, even though it is expressed in nonconventional ways.

RLM is an office manager whose employer is stable but on his own admission not as organized as his many responsibilities require him to be. His chief associate is highly relational and not well organized at all. Both are grateful to have RLM exercise her tight control over details and program procedures to keep the many facets of the business working smoothly.

KV is a church business manager who keeps the church's finances under tight control and effectively maintains good financial procedures for the congregation. This often means that he must (or believes he must) find ways of discouraging the principal pastor from launching enterprises until there is a sound financial base. For other staff members, he often appears to be a hurdle which they must either surmount or avoid. His advice to them is: "When you come to me with a request for more money, have your facts and your reasons clearly outlined. You might be surprised what I will do in responding to your requests for more money if you will only take time to make a good case for them."

Former Secretary of State Henry Kissinger carried out his responsibilities with many of the characteristics of Pattern Two strengths. John Foster Dulles in the 1950s, as Secretary of State, seemed to be running about the world without always knowing what he was about; Mr. Kissinger, on the other hand, always seemed to know precisely where he should be and what he should do. Although he played the role of conciliator in many situations, it was with a sense of control. In his highly structured manner of working, he gained the respect if not always the love of much of the world. His public statements were controlled, thoughtfully explained, and rather dully presented. One always felt that he was sure of his position and of himself.

Significantly, news commentators in comparing his successor Cyrus Vance with Kissinger acknowledged that the work of the State Department would probably not be as well controlled under Vance, but they added that there would be greater openness and public knowledge of what was being done.

Certain common characteristics emerge from these cases: the ability to keep control of one's self, of a situation, and in some instances of others; a tendency not to waste words; and a certainty and sense of conviction that may lead to the temptation to be dogmatic. It is not by chance that in the days when the Bi/Polar System was restricted to business people, the name given to Pattern Two was "control manager." There is in most of the cases a lack of open communication that may lead the person to seem "distant." They also demonstrate the function of the realistic, independent thinker—the one who maintains order where others are either less realistic and/or less disciplined in their dealing with human situations.

Pattern Three—Theoretical and Cooperative

Major strengths are: *Bi/Polar Thinking, Theoretical Thinking,* and *Dependent Risking.* The least strength is Independent Risking.

Typical characteristics are: they tend to be philosophical, articulate, quiet, intellectual, refined, theoretical, orderly, abstract, accepting, dutiful; to avoid conflict; to be naive, learned, organized, shy, thin-skinned, considerate, cultured, sensitive; to understand abstract concepts; to be idealistic, dependable, academic; to hide their feelings; to be soft-spoken, gentle, introspective, scholarly; to live in the world of ideas; to be knowledgable.

ME (see page 48), married to a clergyman, has dealt all her life with the inclination to imagine that things are worse than they are, and to be introspective. "One of the most oppressive fears I had when I married a minister," she writes, "was that I felt I could never 'measure up' as a preacher's wife." Her tendency, like many Pattern Ones and Threes, was to think negatively about herself, and to image herself as someone other than who she was, usually what she thought others wanted her to be. When she finally gave up trying to be that mythical person, she found much more acceptance than previously. Now people often say to her, "You are an ideal minister's wife."

Recently her father, with whom she was quite close, died. In commenting on her struggle with grief, she writes: "You can understand how you can let an idea take hold and overwhelm you."

She is deliberately seeking outlets for her Theoretical Thinking strength rather than dwelling on her grief. She also shows considerable dependence on her husband for assurance as she writes about her struggle.

LR is president of a small company. His great strengths in his business are his ability to keep new ideas flowing into it and his willingness to depend on others to complement his strengths. His greatest problem is in making decisions and following through with things that must be done to keep the business healthy.

In a Bi/Polar Seminar, I asked him how he had been able as a theoretical, dependent thinker to carry on a successful business. "Oh," he said without hesitation, "that's easy to explain. I have two assistants whose responsibility it is to see that I do the things I must do and to carry on the day-by-day practical operational procedures which I don't like to carry out."

JN is a clergyman whose sermons are beautifully thought-out discourses that deal with a wide range of human problems. His use of the Bible is extensive, sound, and helpful. His preaching style is pedantic, sometimes dull, with little flair. In a denomination usually considered more emotionally than intellectually oriented, he has attracted a group that responds to his atypical approach. With this group he has been highly successful, and he has risen rapidly in his denomination. When one of his children died quite young, he responded with open, intellectually honest, and searching sermons (later published in book form). In response to my own grief, which I had to work through on an intellectual as well as a feeling level, I found the sermons as helpful as anything I read.

I should not have been surprised when I heard recently that he had resigned from a prestigious church to take a much smaller one so that he would have more time to devote to his writing.

JA is a student whom I have had in several classes. He is fascinated with ideas but so unsure of himself that he speaks reluctantly even in a small class. In one course he was unable to satisfy himself with his term paper and only because I gave him an extension of time did he pass the course. He solicits my comments on his work, and he is surprised and grateful when I approve of what he has done.

His term paper in a certain course was one of the half dozen or so best prepared I have received in many years of teaching. The ideas were not new, but he had thought them out so well that he produced a paper of both depth and beauty. Like many with Pattern Three strengths, he is able to write more ably than to speak his ideas.

President Woodrow Wilson was probably a Pattern Three. Although educated for law, his early career was as a teacher and writer. He taught at Bryn Mawr, Wesleyan in Connecticut, and Princeton University. After winning an enviable reputation as a teacher, he later served as President of Princeton for eight years. As Governor of New Jersey, he became an active reformer.

Elected President in 1912, he turned his attention to reform and showed remarkable skill in guiding the nation in that direction. During his second term, he worked actively on the project he deemed most important, mediation in the European war in an attempt to bring the two parties together. After this mediation failed, he reluctantly made the decision to declare war. As Arthur S. Link, Professor of History and Director of the Woodrow Wilson Papers at Princeton University, puts it, he "made his greatest contribution in formulating war aims that for the first time gave meaning to the conflict." [7] The treaty which followed the war was a mixture of "Wilsonian idealism and European so-called realism," according to Professor Link. Out of the war he forged the idea of the League of Nations, but he was never able to persuade the Senate to accept the League as he envisioned it.

Two sentences from Link describe the character of President Wilson: "He had a quick and orderly mind and a rare ability to cut through the maze of details to the essence of a subject . . . . He was utterly dependent upon love and friendship, but he perhaps demanded too much of his friends and did not take lightly what he regarded as betrayal of trust." [8]

These people indicate in all instances a love of and ability to deal with ideas, usually with an accompanying idealism (such as that demonstrated especially by President Wilson). Several indicate a greater natural ability to communicate through writing than speaking. There is also a thread of dependency running through them, often shown in the desire for approval and encouragement. There is usually (though not all these cases show it) a problem of self-esteem and a negative self-image.

PATTERN FOUR—INVENTIVE AND INDEPENDENT

Major strengths are: *Bi/Polar Thinking, Theoretical Thinking,* and *Independent Risking.* The least strength is Dependent Risking.

Typical characteristics are: they tend to be imaginative, intelligent, philosophical, theoretical; to discover new ideas; to be perfectionists, idealistic, ingenious, shy, individual-

---

[7] Arthur S. Link, "Wilson, (Thomas) Woodrow," in *Encyclopedia Americana* (1966 Edition) (New York: Americana Corporation, 1966), p. 10.

[8] *Ibid.,* p. 7.

istic, gadgeteers, reserved, sensitive, original, introspective, loners, reflective, rebels, naive, radical; to question established theories; to be self-sufficient; to avoid relationships; to be creative "lone wolves," insightful, subjective, innovators, introvertive, abstract; to follow their own convictions.

AL is a teacher who admits that her greatest problem is in doing what others expect of her, and her greatest delight is in following her own inclination toward creativity. She has found it difficult to accept her husband's natural tendency to work through details, to become successful through a "plodding" approach to his work, and to want to do things "by the book" and to discourage her innovations.

When I observed the two in a Bi/Polar Seminar, AL tried, fairly successfully, to stay with the expectations placed upon seminar leaders to present the ideas and use the procedures of the System. At times she broke out of the mold, however, and began to be herself as she ranged beyond the plan for the seminar. At these times she became animated and obviously enjoyed what she was doing. Occasionally her husband intervened to help get her back on track.

AN was reared in an atmosphere where girls and women were expected to be demure, submissive, dependent, and practical. None of these qualities were natural with her, but she obediently sought to conform to the image imposed upon her. As a consequence in her mature years she has had great difficulty in understanding her true individuality.

Her professional career has consisted of a series of attempts to find a satisfactory way of expressing her naturally imaginative, creative mind, and her independence. She has most often been forced into the role of secretary, and as a consequence has found other outlets for her independent creativity. This has involved the design of an imaginative house, the development of a private business in her spare time, and the pursuit of an academic career completely apart from her usual pursuits. As her husband once said, "When she gets an idea, she becomes literally sick until she finds a way of expressing it."

J. W. Thomas, the originator of the Bi/Polar System, could have remained a management consultant, but his creative and independent mind would not tolerate such restrictions. As he worked with people, the ideas of the Bi/Polar System emerged, and his commitment to them increasingly led him to sacrifice his financial security for the sake of his ideas. He continues his work as a consultant as a means of supporting his thinking.

His temptation is to cut himself off from people and live with his ideas alone. As his System has evolved, however, he has come to see that his thinking is improved as he exposes himself to the critical evaluation of others. "I had had deep convictions of the validity of the Bi/Polar idea almost from the very inception of the ideas," he writes. "The intellectual insights came first, and it was a long time before the emotional and behavioral changes came along." He admits to being an "intuitive thinker"—that is, he thinks ahead of his ability to provide a reasoned explanation of his ideas. Ideas precede the rationale for their meaning.

His greatest problem, Dr. Thomas says, has been the ease with which he can reject others and feel self-confident about doing so. His perception of it preceded his ability to deal with this temptation, but he has increasingly been able to change his feelings and behavior to conform with his ideas. As he has done so, he has been able, often against his basic nature, to become more dependent on others in helping him think through his ideas and to find ways for the practical application of his system.

In his biography of President John Kennedy, Theodore Sorensen calls him "the free man with the free mind." [9] Kennedy wrote his first book, *Why England Slept,* when he was twenty-three years old. Although he was capable of deep commitments, he also retained objectivity—about himself and others. Most people considered him a "liberal," but he never belonged to liberal organizations. As Sorensen puts it, "His most important qualities he had acquired and developed on his own." [10] His wife called him "an idealist without illusions." [11]

It was these qualities that led him during his first months as President to project an innovative program which he believed would be of benefit both to individuals and the nation. Few of these programs were implemented prior to the assassination. One of the exceptions was the highly imaginative Peace Corps. President Johnson, the assertive actionist, was able to put into action many of President Kennedy's ideas during the months when he still remained in the shadow of his predecessor. [12]

---

[9] Theodore C. Sorensen, *Kennedy* (New York: Harper & Row, Publishers, 1965), p. 21.

[10] *Ibid.,* p. 18.

[11] *Ibid.,* p. 22.

[12] It has been difficult to find persons with Pattern Four strengths. There are probably not many such people. At least we have had relatively few in Bi/Polar Seminars. Those who begin seminars sometimes do not complete them. My theory, supported by some evidence, is that they tend to become bored with other people's ideas. When I expressed surprise that a woman I had known for many years, with Pattern Four strengths, did stay on, she said: "Oh, I've developed ways of tuning people out when I'm not interested in what they are saying."

The most common characteristic of Pattern Fours is their imaginative, often innovative thinking. They are often impatient with those who are not as imaginative as they are. Although they may train themselves to relate to people, it is not *natural* for them to do so to any extent. They are often "loners," and may even seem unfriendly when they do not intend to be. Their independence is expressed principally in the realm of ideas, however, and they usually need help, which they may be reluctant to accept, in implementing them. Their great gift to others is their ability to project new ways of thinking and being.

PATTERN FIVE—OUTGOING AND PRACTICAL

Major strengths are: *Bi/Polar Risking, Dependent Risking,* and *Practical Thinking.* The least strength is Theoretical Thinking.

Typical characteristics are: they tend to be warm, outgoing, sympathetic; to like people; to be friendly, aggressively helpful, talkative, emotional, likeable, down-to-earth, concerned for others, "soft sellers," practical, service oriented; to inspire trust; to be generous, gregarious, sociable; to live in a world of people; to pour oil on troubled waters; to be coordinators, compromisers, accepting, extrovertive, involved with people, sensitive to the feelings of others; to allow the "heart to rule reason"; to be diplomatic; to like to work with people; to trust others.

RE is one of the people who helped me in developing an earlier version of this book. He is a professional counselor, working especially in group counseling. Pleasant and outgoing, he relates easily to people. Until I came to know him better, I had thought of him as a superficial thinker. Later, I realized that he is able to see the practical implications of a theory and to express them. Although his interest is primarily in their

practical results, his understanding is far deeper than I had thought.

I also discovered that he could take my naturally turgid prose and turn it into down-to-earth statements, by the addition of illustrative material. His syntax was not always perfect, but it did communicate.

He has problems with his self-image but does not dwell on this tendency; rather, he gets on with his work and is brought back to a better self-image by a pleasant encounter with another person.

CR is a college student whose rebellion during her high school days once made me consider her much more independent than I now recognize her to be. Her practical dependence showed itself in her middle teens as she began to work for long hours and often without financial compensation with young people in the drug culture. Her willingness to come to the aid of some person with a drug problem, I now realize, was not the result of *independence* but instead her tendency *to offer help* to others who needed it regardless of the inconvenience.

She also has trouble with her self-image and may become involved in situations and with persons because of her need for approval. She is quite vulnerable in her relationships and is sometimes hurt by others because of her unrealistic expectations of them.

KM is a superior leader of groups who relates to people naturally and warmly so as to inspire both a positive and deep response. In his presentation of the Bi/Polar System, he is better at telling a story that illustrates a point than at explaining ideas. His presentation has a kind of "sparkle" to it because of this ability to use narrative material and to communicate enthusiasm and warmth. One gets the impression that he is personally involved with each member of the group. His contribution to the team with which he works, the other two members of which are less warm, is in his ability to create a relaxed atmosphere in groups.

PW is an articulate, outgoing church professional who first saw herself as more independent than dependent. She later realized that this conclusion was based on the fact that she had been forced early in her marriage to support both herself and her family. Her practicality had led her to express her relational nature in an assertive and positive manner in order to achieve her goal of being a responsible parent alone.

She has been unusually successful in her work because of the warm relationships she has with others and her expression of these relationships in a dependent but not overly-dependent manner. Her personality "sparkles," and she brings life to a group. In her work with church volunteers, she is able to communicate her enthusiasm and to make it clear that she is depending on them to do the job they agreed to fulfill.

Former President Gerald Ford has the natural strengths of the Pattern Five, though increasingly during his presidency he exercised the functions of the office by providing a more dynamic kind of leadership. Part of this was his ability to inspire love and confidence in his more dynamic associates.

The clue to his basic pattern of strengths can be seen in his close relationship with other members of the Congress during his years as a part of that body. According to newscasters who spoke of this relationship as he prepared to leave the presidential office, his farewell to that body when he became vice president was a tearful one. Scarcely less so was his farewell as he vacated the presidential office. Both those who agreed and those who disagreed with him joined in this general feeling of warmth toward him as a person.

Apparently the American public also saw him as a warm person. In the conclusions drawn from the final Gallup Poll made shortly before the end of his term as President is the statement that "he increased the morale of the nation, restored confidence in the presidency, and created greater unity among the American people." [13] These are typical fruits of Pattern Five strengths.

The most common characteristic of these Pattern Five cases is the warm and close relationships which they have or can establish with people. Generally they are not as much concerned with theories as they are with their practical implications. Often their contribution to others is the ability to be a reconciler. Almost invariably they enjoy the confidence of others and naturally draw others to themselves. In many situations, their temptation is to let others rule their lives.

PATTERN SIX—OUTGOING AND INTUITIVE

Major strengths are: *Bi/Polar Risking, Dependent Risking,* and *Theoretical Thinking.* The least strength is Practical Thinking.

Typical characteristics are: they tend to be diplomatic, outgoing, sociable, emotionally expressive; to have a flair for the dramatic; to be joiners, idealistic, witty; to have a feel for people; to be abstract, optimistic, excitable, changeable, talkative, romantic, flamboyant, uninhibited; to allow the heart to rule reason; to be warm, accepting; to have cultural interests; to like to work with groups; to be extroverts, subjective; to live in the world of people;

---

[13] As reported in *The Dallas Morning News,* Sunday, January 16, 1977, Section A, p. 14.

to be performers, aggressive in relationships; to "wear their heart on their sleeve"; to be imaginative, intuitive.

CM is a scintillating young matron who looks and acts far younger than the age of her children proves her to be. When her husband completed an advanced degree, she did a thoroughly impractical but equally delightful thing by inviting all his friends to a gala celebration dinner. (It was impractical because of the cost involved and the condition of the family's finances.) Sixty people showed up for the catered dinner! During the celebration she recognized each person by name and commended them for contributions they had made to her husband's successful completion of his academic program.

After his resumption of his profession, she enrolled in college to complete her degree and prepare for a career in counseling that will necessitate an advanced degree. At one point, she felt rejection from her counseling instructor because of his disagreement with some of her ideas. A few months later she and her husband had become intimate friends of the teacher and his wife, developing what she called a "one to one relationship that allows mutual sharing of ideas."

CM, like most Pattern Sixes, brings vivacity, optimism, and delight wherever she goes.

When GN walked into a Bi/Polar seminar, I immediately spotted him as a Pattern Six. It was not just that he spoke personally to each person in the group—that could have been learned behavior, since he was the associate pastor of the church where the seminar was being conducted. Rather, it was the fact that he was obviously taking such delight in what he was doing.

When his Bi/Polar inventory later confirmed my guess, I asked him if he played a musical instrument or enjoyed some other form of enter-

taining others. (Those with Pattern Six strengths
often do.) He at first denied that he was an enter-
tainer. Later he somewhat sheepishly admitted:
"I wasn't quite truthful with you. Actually I play
the bagpipes and do magic tricks."

His wife had trouble in determining what her
strengths were. "I don't really think I'm practical," she observed, "but I've had to learn how
to be to make up for the fact that GN has so little
concern for practical matters." We eventually
concluded that she was a Pattern Eight.

LT is a clergyman with high relational and theoretical strength. Although well-liked by those
who knew him, he had never quite "got things
together" as he approached his 40s. This was
partly due to a low self-image created by an un-
distinguished record in school. There had been
too many people to enjoy and too many diverting
experiences for him to bother much with his
studies. He admits that when he came to his first
Bi/Polar seminar, he did not know how much he
was overdrawn at the bank!

Those who knew him would never have
guessed that he was not a fully integrated person. His outgoing, friendly nature made him everyone's friend. The Bi/Polar System has helped
him express his Practical Thinking and Independent Risking strengths without losing his naturally outgoing response to other people. His life
has taken on new purpose, and as he has demonstrated his ability to deal more constructively
with his work, he has been given greater responsibilities.

President Theodore Roosevelt exemplifies
many of the characteristics of a Pattern Six. Although we normally think of him as a swash-
buckling, daring fighter, this appears to have
been more the public image than the real Theodore Roosevelt. He is described by one of his
biographers, Edward Wagenknecht, as being

"most charming of all in his family relationships." [14] Joseph Lash in *Eleanor and Franklin* quotes his daughter Alice as saying he had a "tribal affection" shown by his love for his large family, including nephews and nieces. [15] His contributions to others, never exploited for publicity purposes, were also numerous outside his family. In one incident, at the height of his career, he took a crying baby from the arms of her mother on a train and walked the aisle until the baby fell asleep. He did not cherish his disagreements, and he was witty and capable of humorous sayings that people remembered long after more sober pronouncements were forgotten. As Wagenknecht puts it, "Few presidents have sought advice so freely and widely." [16] His compassion for people was considerable, and his weakest point is usually considered to be his failure to deal adequately with the economic interests of the country.

In short, he is described as being a "vivid and dominating personality," with everything he did considered exciting. [17]

Mark Twain (Samuel L. Clemens) was certainly a Pattern Six personality. His humor is best known from his writing; it was also evident, even early in life, in his personal relationships. He chose the name "Mark Twain" from a river term that means "two fathoms, safe water." His wife Olivia Langdon is described as "the steadying and restraining influence her husband needed." [18]

[14] Edward Wagenknecht, "Roosevelt, Theodore," *Encyclopedia Americana*, 1966 edition (New York: Americana Corporation, 1966), Vol. 23, p. 686a.

[15] Joseph P. Lash, *Eleanor and Franklin* (New York: W. W. Norton & Company, 1971), p. 72.

[16] Wagenknecht, *op. cit.*, p. 696a.

[17] *Ibid.*, p. 685.

[18] DeLancey Ferguson, "Clemens, Samuel Langhorne," *Encyclopedia Americana*, 1966 edition (New York: Americana Corporation, 1966), Vol. 7, p. 85.

On two occasions his speculation brought financial ruin, a result of unwise (impractical?)
ventures. His speculative nature was also expressed in his writing, and in his later years it led
to the development of a unique, mechanistically
oriented philosophy.[19] Although his fiction also
showed great imagination, he attributed his ability to draw vivid personality pictures in his stories
to the warm, personal interest that he took in
people.[20]

Typical Pattern Six characteristics are clear from these
cases—deep, warm relationships with people, often mani-
fest in concern for their welfare; charm and vivacity in
their relationships; humor and the ability to bring joy to
others. They often develop some form of structured ability to entertain—as story tellers, practical jokers, popular
musicians, and the like. Their lack of practicality sometimes leads to problems, as does their trust in others. Perhaps their mission in life is to provide zest for those who
lack it, who in turn provide a steadying influence for those
with Pattern Six strengths.

PATTERN SEVEN—ASSERTIVE AND ENTERPRISING

Major strengths are: *Bi/Polar Risking, Independent
Risking,* and *Practical Thinking.* The least strength is
Theoretical Thinking.

Typical characteristics are: Sevens tend to be self-
starters, forceful, self-confident, competitive, ambitious,
dynamic, resourceful; to have a high drive; to be actionists,
enthusiastic, practical, independent, hard drivers, impetuous, impatient; to stimulate change; to seek freedom and
power; to be aggressive, individualistic, self-reliant, enterprising, debaters; to lift themselves up "by their own boot-

---

[19] *Loc. cit.*
[20] Ferguson, *op. cit.,* p. 84.

straps"; to be realistic; to take calculated risks; to be activators, outspoken; to take the initiative; to be self-assertive; to follow their own convictions.

DW is a clergyman who was appointed pastor of a church that has had a long-time reputation as being difficult to serve. Its history has indicated a conservative stance toward change, and a tendency to take a critical, carping attitude toward its pastoral leadership. DW has not allowed this history to deter him in his dynamic leadership. During his pastorate, attendance at worship has increased dramatically, and a steady influx of younger families has changed the character of the church. Older members disapprove of some of his actions but are quick to defend and support him. Not only has the membership increased, but also the budget. Art glass windows have been added to the sanctuary; a Vietnamese family was sponsored and supported by the congregation; and an extensive building program was launched successfully. Even when he has assigned more routine matters, such as pastoral calling, to an assistant, he has been able to maintain a high level of acceptance by a congregation that once considered this the most important work of the pastor.

EW is a dynamic person who was employed as a secretary but soon was made administrative assistant. Since the head of the department was also dynamic, there were sometimes problems between the two, and EW was required to assume more of the stabilizing role than is natural for her, with little satisfaction in doing so. During an absence of the department head, an idea-centered person assumed some of his responsibilities. His way of working was to plan with EW and then depend upon her to carry most of the responsibilities for implementation.

EW later resigned and resumed her academic training. She has since become the head of another enterprise that is moving forward under her leadership. Her only problem is that her assertiveness sometimes expresses itself in an abrasive manner that arouses criticism from those dependent on her services.

Even as a child it was John who provided the leadership for those with whom he played. As a high school student in a highly competitive school, his combination of dynamic leadership and his frustrations at not being able to exercise that leadership fully led to a stage where he was sometimes considered a "bully." In college he rose to leadership in his fraternity and became its president, and his "cockiness" began to disappear.

Instead of accepting a salaried position after college, he and a stable friend began their own business. The business has grown in spite of considerable competition from more established enterprises. His marriage to a relationally oriented, highly committed Christian young woman has provided a balance to John's independence in his home as his business partner has provided stability in his business.

Two U.S. presidents within recent history provide examples of dynamic persons. Harry Truman, thrust into the presidential office by the death of Franklin Roosevelt, was supposed to become a weak and ineffective president. Instead, he adjusted quickly to the demands of the office and made such difficult decisions as the use of the atomic bomb, the relieving of General Douglas MacArthur from his postwar command of the occupation forces in Japan, and the establishing of a vigorous policy to counteract the increasing influence of Soviet Russia in Western Europe. President Truman's philosophy was, "When I make a decision, I don't worry about it. I get a good night's sleep so I'll be ready for the next day's problems."

President Lyndon Johnson was also a dynamic person. During the first months of his presidency, he was able to get through Congress many of the programs which his predecessor, John Kennedy, had conceived but had not been able to implement. In the later years of his Presidency, he either misjudged the mood of the country, acted on his convictions regardless of their growing unpopularity, or began to enjoy the power of the presidency too much. Historians have not yet sorted out all the factors involved. Whatever the causes, his escalation of the Vietnam war led to sufficient negative reaction that he decided—and announced dramatically—not to seek a second full term.

Betty Ford, the wife of former President Gerald Ford, often acted like a Pattern Seven. (Her total personality is still too much in question for a complete assessment of it to be made.) Her expression of her own point of view even when it was unpopular, and the practical and open way in which she faced her cancer are two examples. President Ford's support of her in both of these situations is another indication of the strong Pattern Five component in his personality.

It is difficult to determine whether Eleanor Roosevelt was a Pattern Two who later found ways of expressing all her strengths or a Pattern Seven whose childhood pressed her into a Pattern Two mold. On the basis of Joseph P. Lash's book I have concluded that the overwhelming evidence is that the latter is the case. As a single example supporting this conclusion, Lash quotes from a letter written by Mlle. Souvestre, headmistress of the London school Allenswood, to which Eleanor was sent when she was fifteen

years old. Mlle. Souvestre wrote: "I have not
found her easily influenced in anything that was
not perfectly straightforward and honest, but I
often found she influenced others in the right
direction." [21]
The "emergence of Eleanor Roosevelt," as
Lash calls Part III of his book based on her private papers, was long and often painful. As she
later put it, "As life developed, I faced each problem as it came along . . . . When I found something to do—I just did it." [22] The latter years of her
life are too familiar to most Americans to require
retelling.

It appears that Cissy Patterson, publisher of
the *Washington Herald,* was correct in saying of
Eleanor Roosevelt that she was "a complete ex-
trovert, of course." [23]

Dynamic, enterprising, and practical are three of the
common threads running through these Pattern Seven
cases. They are people who express convictions, provide
natural leadership, and accomplish what others may find
it difficult to do. When such qualities are undisciplined or
the situation itself does not provide checks, they may
eventuate in a love of power and its abuse. Pattern Sevens
are actionists, the doers, the movers of society. American
society has tended to exalt and glamorize such persons
among men, has often discouraged women from asserting
the same qualities, and has sometimes failed to recognize
that other qualities are equally valuable.

PATTERN EIGHT—DYNAMIC AND PERSUASIVE

Major strengths are: *Bi/Polar Risking, Independent
Risking,* and *Theoretical Thinking.* The least strength is
Practical Thinking.

----

[21] Lash, *op. cit.,* p. 74.
[22] *Ibid.,* p. 378.
[23] *Loc. cit.*

Typical characteristics are: they tend to be dynamic, persuasive, forceful, idealistic, self-starters, self-confident, aggressive; to have an intuitive feel; to be competitive; to see the potential; to be pioneers of ideas, visionary; to have explosive personalities; to make a strong emotional impact; to possess an active imagination; to be optimistic, impetuous, emotionally involved; to have magnetic personalities; to be irrepressible, colorful, spellbinders, promoters, risk takers, enthusiastic, bored with details, charming, attracted by possibilities, subjective, stimulators of change.

WB became president of a small college whose future was extremely doubtful. Its enrollment had been declining, its financial status was in jeopardy, and those of its faculty who had not departed were demoralized. Many questioned the need for such a college, and its purpose was unclear.

In the course of a few years, WB completely reversed these trends. Enrollment increased; he secured money to initiate new programs with first-rate leadership; morale has never been higher; and the purpose of the college has been redefined.

All of this has occurred because WB brought dynamic and imaginative leadership to the situation. He has been able to attract faculty and administrative leadership of high quality, some of whom have left secure and prestigious positions to become a part of the school's "team." "Bold" is the only word to use in describing his financial policy, both in spending and in soliciting funds. Fortunately, a Pattern Two business manager keeps the President from overextending the school's resources irresponsibly. In relation to all of this an extensive promotional campaign has changed the public image of the school and made possible a long-range financial plan that seems likely to secure the school's future.

ET is a young matron who for several years has managed her home, including three young children; taught part-time in a junior college; and pursued a graduate degree on a part-time basis. She is both dynamic and imaginative with a tendency to project grandiose enterprises which as often as not she is able to carry through. She has learned to consult with others who both help her to be more realistic about what can be done and at the same time provide support in the implementation of her ideas.

In one instance she conceived a plan for which she needed the support of community leaders, mostly male. In an initial meeting she "sold" the group on the idea and secured both their support and assistance in carrying out the project. ET has boundless energy and enthusiasm, and she is able to instill in others some measure of these qualities.

DB is a mature woman married to an assertive and enterprising man in whose shadow she has tended to live. Because she has played her role so well, even one of her children failed to perceive her dynamic nature when he completed her Bi/Polar inventory of strengths. Her dynamic and imaginative qualities have made her a skilled teacher of children with learning disabilities, and she has transferred these skills to an undertaking with adults whose reading ability is as low as grade three. Often she is able to increase their ability several grades in a four weeks' program.

At the end of a Bi/Polar seminar, she said to the leader, "My, it's great to be able to really *be* a Pattern Eight without trying to pretend to be someone else!"

Martin Luther King, Jr., was undoubtedly a Pattern Eight. After earning a Ph.D. degree from Boston University, he came to national recognition when he led the successful boycott of segregated busing in Montgomery, Alabama, in 1956. During the next eight years, by using a policy of nonviolent resistance, he faced the ire of many whites by his demand for equal rights for blacks, and of some blacks for his refusal to resort to violence. In spite of many arrests, physical attacks, and verbal abuse, he rallied his people, as well as many whites, to the cause of racial justice and began a nonviolent change in American society that has continued after his assassination in 1968. His strengths were always complemented by others who handled details.

His dynamic and imaginative character is perhaps best symbolized in his rallying speech to 200,000 civil rights marchers in Washington in August 1963. Its recurring theme, "I have a dream," and the ringing quality of his delivery, since repeated many times on television, are typical results of Pattern Eight strengths.

President Franklin Roosevelt also demonstrated many Pattern Eight characteristics. Joseph Lash records an incident about him at five years of age when he responded to his mother's dominant control with the words, "Oh for freedom." [24] Lash calls him independent and self-reliant,[25] inclined in his young years to cockiness. He writes of Eleanor Roosevelt's recognition during the early years of their marriage of his tendency to "be egocentric and impulsive." [26]

Assuming the presidency when the United States was on the brink of financial collapse, he began a program that was at best imaginative, at its worst reckless. His first inaugural address, which he had written himself the previous Sunday, began with his ringing voice carried across

[24] Lash, *op. cit.*, p. 117.
[25] *Ibid.*, p. 119.
[26] *Ibid.*, p. 120.

the nation by radio, "Let me first assert my firm
belief that the only thing we have to fear is fear
itself . . . ."
William Manchester describes his first hundred days in office as being a time of improvisa-
tion. " 'Take a method and try it,' he told his New
Dealers. 'If it fails, try another. But above all, try
something.' " [27] Manchester quotes the eminent
historian Charles A. Beard, no great admirer of
Roosevelt, as saying that he discussed "more
fundamental problems of American life and society than all the other presidents combined." [28]

"Dynamic" and "imaginative" are among the most
common themes in these Pattern Eight cases. "Persuasive"
is another typical characteristic. Called by Dr. Thomas
"the most dynamic of the patterns," Eights both *imagine*
the possibilities that do not now exist and, sometimes impulsively, *move* to carry them through. Often they require
the backing of one or more persons with stronger practical
strength. They can rally others to their cause, however,
and inspire them to do the detail work which Pattern
Eights dislike. They are often effective public speakers.
One of their temptations is to overextend themselves and
refuse to listen to those who reveal the facts of reality to
them.

Problems in Identifying Patterns of Strengths

We have now completed the process of helping you
identify your pattern of strengths. I hope that you are
reasonably comfortable with one of the patterns as your
basic one. If you are not, material in subsequent chapters
may help you in your self-identification. Talking with
another person may also be useful. This may confirm you

---

[27] Manchester, *op. cit.*, Vol. One, p. 95.
[28] *Ibid.*, p. 96.

in your present understanding, alter your self-perception, or aid in your arrival at a decision concerning your basic pattern of strengths.

Some people do not find it easy to identify their pattern. There are several reasons for this difficulty. Not everything we do is an expression of our greater strengths. Human beings are adaptable creatures and therefore learn to do that which does not come easy. Such learning may be deliberate—we *choose* to act in a manner that makes it easier for us to negotiate life in our particular environment. Or it may be reactive—we *react* without realizing fully what we are doing to a set of circumstances in order to survive.

Choosing to emphasize our lesser strengths requires discipline but is not harmful; *being forced to do so* without realizing what is happening may lead to resentment, frustration, and even physical illness. Some women, for example, *choose* to be homemakers as long as they have young children rather than using the full range of their potential; others feel *bound* to do so by cultural expectations and fail to seek fulfillment in voluntary work. Both men and women may feel *trapped* in a job that is not fulfilling; or they may *choose* to remain in the position because they see it as the best alternative. *Awareness* of who one is and the *acceptance* of circumstances that do not lead to fulfilment are the key conditions for dealing with conditions we cannot control.

Sometimes we become so accustomed to acting in a way not compatible with our natural pattern of strengths that we have problems in determining who we really are. Habit is a powerful force, not easily broken. When we come to greater self-understanding, we may still be forced to act in ways not fully to our liking. This self-knowledge can help us become a more relaxed and fulfilled person, however.

On the other hand, knowing who we are can lead us to the knowledge that we all ought to act out of our lesser strengths at times in order to fulfill our responsibilities. For example, parents whose greater strength in Dependent Risking leads them to be naturally permissive may come to see that they need to emphasize their Independent Risking to provide the firm and consistent adult whom their children need.

"Blending"

This process of adaptation is the conscious or unconscious expression of a *blend* of our natural pattern of strengths. We learn to emphasize one of our lesser strengths to a greater degree than our natural inclination. Although we are really all a Pattern Nine, with our own unique blending of our natural strengths, a Pattern One remains a *Basic* Pattern One even when he/she learns to emphasize Independent Risking in order to take charge of a situation that requires someone to be in control.

I have recently learned the joy of using a modern food blender with its neat variety of speeds and its array of "buttons" to produce them. Not long ago I wanted to make a cheese ball, and I chose a recipe whose basic ingredient was Cheddar cheese. I also used blue and cream cheese as well as other ingredients, and these changed the flavor but not the basic quality of the Cheddar cheese. The cheese ball was still essentially Cheddar.

This is essentially what we mean when we talk about personality blends. My basic "flavor" as a person is a dependent, theoretical thinker. I am most at home in dealing with ideas, especially in writing. My inclination is to explain an idea and then, perhaps, to illustrate it. In this book I have sometimes deliberately followed a different approach and have begun with an illustration and then explained what it means. Story telling is not natural for me, but I can do it. When I follow the story approach, I am using a blend of my basic pattern of strengths. It is no doubt obvious to those stronger in Risking strength, how-ever, that I have maintained rather consistently my ten-dency to explain ideas rather than to narrate a story.

A "pattern blend" in Bi/Polar terms means that we emphasize a lesser strength more than is natural for us. My basic Pattern Three means that it is not easy for me to be the genial host. I do not enter into "small talk" readily nor am I really very good at it. My wife is usually the one who carries the major load in entertaining friends. When she is not present, however, I find that I can re-spond to the situation, use my lesser strengths, and do a reasonably adequate job of being the host.

The fact that I have used my lesser strengths does not mean that my basic pattern has changed. I am still a Pat-tern Three in my strengths, but I have used my strengths with a different slant. As a consequence I may *seem* to have become a Pattern Five or Six, but I have not. By emphasizing my Risking strengths, I have become a *Warm Three*, and my Pattern Three has been blended with a Pattern Six.

Pattern Blends

Each pattern of strengths has four possible slants. There is the "pure" expression of the basic pattern consisting of those qualities listed for the pattern in an earlier section of this chapter. There are also three blends in which we emphasize one of our lesser strengths, even our least. The well-adapted person learns to shift his/her emphasis ac-cording to what a situation demands. We therefore have learned to use *all* our strengths more creatively.

In outline form the possible blends for each pattern are: [29]

---

[29] For further information on pattern blends, see J. W. Thomas, *Bi/Polar: A Positive Way of Understanding People*, Chap. 8. Dr. Thomas uses the term "Idealistic" where I have used "Theo-retical."

Basic Pattern	Blend	Strength Emphasized	Designation of Blend
1. One	One/Two	Independent Risking	Assertive One
One	One/Three	Theoretical Thinking	Theoretical One
One	One/Five	Dependent Risking	Warm One
2. Two	Two/One	Dependent Risking	Warm Two
Two	Two/Four	Theoretical Thinking	Theoretical Two
Two	Two/Seven	Independent Risking	Assertive Two
3. Three	Three/One	Practical Thinking	Realistic Three
Three	Three/Four	Independent Risking	Assertive Three
Three	Three/Six	Dependent Risking	Warm Three
4. Four	Four/Two	Practical Thinking	Realistic Four
Four	Four/Three	Dependent Risking	Warm Four
Four	Four/Eight	Independent Risking	Assertive Four
5. Five	Five/One	Practical Thinking	Realistic Five
Five	Five/Six	Theoretical Thinking	Theoretical Five
Five	Five/Seven	Independent Risking	Assertive Five
6. Six	Six/Three	Theoretical Thinking	Theoretical Six
Six	Six/Five	Practical Thinking	Realistic Six
Six	Six/Eight	Independent Risking	Assertive Six
7. Seven	Seven/Two	Practical Thinking	Realistic Seven
Seven	Seven/Five	Dependent Risking	Warm Seven
Seven	Seven/Eight	Theoretical Thinking	Theoretical Seven
8. Eight	Eight/Four	Theoretical Thinking	Theoretical Eight
Eight	Eight/Six	Dependent Risking	Warm Eight
Eight	Eight/Seven	Practical Thinking	Realistic Eight

There are no pattern blends other than those listed. For example, there is no One/Seven blend; rather, the Pattern One who acts more like a Seven is using his/her One/Two blend and is therefore being more assertive. The Pattern Seven who seems more like a Pattern Three is using his/her Seven/Eight blend and perhaps the Seven/Five blend and seems to be both more theoretical and more relational. That is, each pattern can emphasize one or more of his/her lesser strengths and *appear to be* like a pattern that is not a possible blend. The *actual* blend is with a pattern whose configuration of strengths is compatible with that of the basic pattern. Nor is the basic pattern lost, as we have noted; an Assertive Two has not become a Pattern Seven but is still a Pattern Two behaving with a Seven slant, or in other words, he is showing Pattern Seven tendencies.

It is possible for us to express at one time or another all three of our pattern blends; usually we operate out of one more often than the other two. For example, my most common blend is the Realistic Three, for the circumstances of my life have encouraged me to be practical. At times I am an Assertive Three, but unless I carefully plan my assertiveness I often regret what I have done. I wish I had self-consciously tried earlier in my life to develop my Three/Six blend more fully, since I think this would have added flair and zest to my personal and professional life. With effort I can act out of my Three/Six blend, but it does not come easily for me.

In any discussion of blends, it is important to emphasize the importance of knowing your *basic* pattern of strengths. This pattern indicates the set of your personality, the most natural way in which you express yourself. Blends are the form and texture of the expression of your major strengths, and you may live out of one blend fairly consistently or it may vary depending on the circumstances. Your basic pattern is the foundation from which you grow into a more creative person and the base for learning to relate with others. An Assertive Five does not become a Pattern Seven, but a Pattern Five whose Independent Risking is being used more fully.

This chapter has been concerned with two purposes of the book: understanding yourself and others. Subsequent chapters will deal with the other two purposes: your personal growth and the improvement of your relationships with other people.

Discussion and Activity Guide

1. Study the tendencies and temptations in the Appendix as a further aid in determining your major strengths. Note the footnotes that suggest the tendencies and temptation most common for particular strengths.
2. If you are still uncertain about your basic pattern of strengths, review the words and phrases characteristic of each

pattern that may be your own. Try to be realistic about yourself in this process. If there is no one pattern where you have underlined at least one-half of the words, review the three chapters that deal with the three pairs of strengths.

3. Review the pattern blends. Possible blends for each pattern are:

Basic Pattern	Possible Blends
One	Two, Three, Five
Two	One, Four, Seven
Three	One, Four, Six
Four	Two, Three, Eight
Five	One, Six, Seven
Six	Three, Five, Eight
Seven	Two, Five, Eight
Eight	Four, Six, Seven

4. Underline words and phrases characteristic of each of your possible blends to determine what blend or blends you most often use.

5. Write on your worksheet your basic pattern and your most common blend or blends.

6. What blend is most difficult for you to express?

7. Discuss your choices with one or more people.

Part II

Using Your Strengths

Creatively

–6–

Foundations for Growth

In a recent seminary class, I asked a group of students to demonstrate the use of body movement as a way of teaching. As is often the case, I learned more from these students than I had been able to teach them.

The leader of the group asked us to sit on the floor. "Although we are going to pray, I want you to keep your eyes open," he told us. "Make a tight fist, raise your arm to chest height, and hold your hands and arms as rigidly as possible."

As we sat with arms outstretched, each hand held in a rigid fist, our knuckles began to turn white and our arms began to grow weary. The voice of the leader, in a prayer of confession, reminded us of our tendency to hold ourselves back from meaningful relationships as we keep our deepest feelings inside and become more and more uptight. Seated in the circle was a former medical student from Nepal, a Korean student still struggling with the vagaries of the English language, a former Muslim from Nigeria, a young American whose theological convictions conflicted with the prevailing ideology of the school, an older student seeking a new life after a serious and near fatal life-error, and others of whose inner struggles I was only dimly aware.

We were told to open our fists gradually and relax our arms as a symbol of our open relationships with others and with God. Finally, we joined hands in the circle and the prayer ended.

We were not asked to reveal our inner secrets, nor did the circumstances of our lives change because of this single experience. There was a new feeling among us, however, and individually and corporately we were made new by reaching out to one another, symbolized by the simple movement of hands and arms.

In one sense nothing was changed, and yet something important happened. The situations in which we lived, the problems and frustrations we faced, were not altered. Our attitude toward them and toward one another was.

The prayer used by Alcoholics Anonymous is a parable of life as well as a prayer: "Lord, help me to change those things that I can change, to accept those things that I cannot, and to be able to tell the difference between the two."

Self-help systems abound in our time. Some of them offer the illusion that if we will only repeat a secret formula or engage in a particular exercise, all will be well. But life is not that simple, and problems do not go away so easily. If we are to live creatively, we must be able to distinguish between those things we *can* change and those we can*not*.

The purpose of this chapter is to make this distinction, and to suggest other foundations of the Bi/Polar process of growth.

The first assumption that operates in this process is what we have already noted: *There are some things about our lives that we can change and others that we cannot change.*

One life force that does not change is our individuality.[1]

---

[1] These "life forces" are taken directly from Dr. Thomas's work. See *Bi/Polar: A Positive Way of Understanding People*, Chap. 7. Used by permission.

By individuality I mean our particular arrangement of the three pairs of polar strengths—Bi/Polar Thinking and Risking, Practical and Theoretical Thinking, and Dependent and Independent Risking. We can use the strengths either creatively or destructively; their basic pattern, however, is the God-given core of our personality.

Three historical religious leaders illustrate how individuality remains constant even when its specific expressions change.

Moses was a prince in the court of the Pharaoh but aware of his Hebrew parentage. One day his sympathy for his own people was aroused, and in anger he killed an Egyptian taskmaster. Not a revolutionary, he fled to the land of Midian when he realized that his deed had been discovered.

In the land of Midian his sympathetic relationship with other people led to his protecting the daughters of the priest and his subsequent marriage to one of the daughters. In the desert as he kept watch over his father-in-law's sheep, he had a vivid experience of God at the "burning bush." This changed the direction of his life, and he began to understand God's call to free the Hebrew people from bondage.

But Moses protested and found excuses for not accepting the call. "I am a halting speaker," he said (Exodus 6:30, *New English Bible*). Finally, with his brother Aaron as his mouthpiece, he reluctantly accepted the challenge. During his dealings with the Pharaoh, he showed remarkable restraint and persistence, and in the subsequent attempts to mold an integrated people out of a group of runaway Hebrew slaves the same qualities usually served him well. Occasionally his anger would surface, as it did at Mt. Sinai when he broke the tablets of the law.

Moses gradually gained more self-confidence as his dependence on God grew stronger, and Aaron disappears in the record as his spokesman. A more dynamic leader might have forced the Hebrew people into unwilling compliance; Moses, however, guided them with a careful concern for

human and physical logistics. He was the law-giver, the
stabilizer, forced against his desire to assume leadership.
And it was his more dynamic successor, Joshua, who led
the people across the Jordan to begin the conquest of the
land of Canaan.

In terms of the illustrations in Chapter 5, Moses was
more like Eisenhower (Pattern One) than Patton or
Montgomery (Patterns Seven). He remained the stable
law-giver throughout his life, and God was able to use his
essentially low-key leadership to effect his purposes.

A more obvious example is the apostle Paul. Before his
conversion to Christianity, Paul (or Saul, the Jewish name
by which he was first known) was a dynamic, hard-driving,
self-confident, charismatic Pharisee. (See, for example,
Acts 9:1,2, 1 Corinthians 15:9, and Galatians 1:13,14.)
After his conversion to Christianity, he was a dynamic,
hard-driving, self-confident, charismatic Christian. (In
other words, his strengths were those of a Pattern Eight.)
This latter part of Paul's life can be seen in such passages
as 2 Corinthians 10:1–18, Galatians 2:11–21, and 2 Thes-
salonians 3:6–12. His direction in life was radically
changed; his basic individuality was not.

Augustine of Hippo (A.D. 354–430) spent his early life
moving from one philosophical system to another, finally
gravitating to Platonic philosophy. Never quite satisfied
with any of them, he finally embraced Christianity and
became one of the chief architects of its theology not only
for his time but for the centuries following. Both the
character of his life and the content of his thinking
changed, but he remained essentially a thinker and writer,
probably a Pattern Three. As one writer puts it, "Augustine's abiding importance rests on his penetrating understanding of Christian truth." [2]

A second life force that does not change is our *inner*

---

[2] *The Oxford Dictionary of the Christian Church*, ed. F. L.
Cross (London: Oxford University Press, 1958, 1961), p. 106.

capacities—physical stamina, energy level, intelligence, native ability, and the like. Some people are just more lavishly endowed by birth than others. For example, I have a sixteen-year-old friend who can sight-read a Beethoven sonata on the piano and a Bach fugue on the organ, and after a few rehearsals perform in an extraordinary manner before an audience. I have another friend whose unbelievably high degree of intelligence, accompanied by a photographic memory, enables him to converse intelligently on almost any topic—from medicine to theology, from nuclear physics to speculative philosophy. And a third friend has such a high level of energy that on one occasion when a group of us who had spent a wearying but fascinating evening in the Philadelphia bicentennial museum began the walk back to our hotel, she went skipping along the top of a garden wall while the rest of us dragged our weary feet along, too tired even to do much talking.

This may all seem unfair, and I must confess to feeling considerable envy at times of those so richly endowed. I find some comfort in Jesus' statement, "Every one to whom much is given, of him will much be required" (Luke 12:48). The comfort does not last for long, however, for I am quickly reminded that I have not used fully what I have been given. And I remember John Baillie's prayer, "God, set me free . . . from thinking lightly of the one talent Thou hast given me, because Thou hast not given me five or ten."[3]

A third life force is the *environment*. We obviously cannot alter our past environment; it, like our individuality and innate capacities, is a given. "What's done is done and can't be undone" is a fact of life. The truth of Edward Fitzgerald's poem, "The Rubiyat of Omar Khayyam," is undeniable:

---

[3] John Baillie, *A Diary of Private Prayer* (New York: Charles Scribner's Sons, 1936), p. 131.

The moving Finger writes, and having writ,
Moves on. Nor all thy Piety nor wit
Shall lure it back to cancel half a line
Nor all thy Tears wash out a Word of it.

To be sure we can change our attitude toward the past, and we can face our mistakes in the knowledge of God's forgiveness. And we *can*, within limits, change the present and the future. Sometimes this means getting out of one situation into another, and at other times it means bringing our own influence to bear on a situation.

The fourth life force—one with which we are much concerned in this book—is personal choice. I shall not join in the long-standing argument concerning *whether* we have freedom, and if so, *how much*. B. F. Skinner and most behavioristic psychologists deny the reality of freedom.[4] Recent studies of the brain, on the other hand, support the notion that there is built into the brain itself the structures which make free decisions possible.[5] Whatever other evidence there is for choice, there is the inescapable *experience of having freedom*, limited though it may be in many situations, and it is this experience which I want to affirm and support.

The heart of the growth process, in fact, is the widening of our ability to make choices that lead to a more constructive coping with life through dealing with our inborn characteristics and outward circumstances. There are two principal ways in which subsequent chapters will provide help in increasing your range of choices. First, they will help you see how you can use all your strengths creatively so that your decisions contribute to maturity. Second, they will encourage, even prod, you to make such choices as

    [4] B. F. Skinner, *Beyond Freedom and Dignity* (Bantam/Vintage Books, 1972), esp. Chaps. 2 and 6.
    [5] See, for example, Roger W. Sperry, "Left-Brain, Right Brain," *Saturday Review*, August 9, 1975, pp. 30–3. Dr. Sperry is Hixon Professor of Psychobiology at the California Institute of Technology.

you deal with yourself and your relationship with God and with other people.

There are some things we cannot change—but there are many we can; and we need to be both realistic and imaginative in deepening our capacity to make choices that lead toward the releasing of our capacity to become a more adequate person.

The second assumption of this chapter is what we have already implied: *we are all endowed with the capacity to become more mature, self-motivated, direction-oriented persons.* Our understanding of what maturity means will depend on our values—our faith, if you will. But all of us are related to Ultimate Creative Strength through creation and have the capacity to use who we are and the circumstances of our lives more constructively. That is, who we become *can* also be a gift from God as we respond to his continued working in and through us to bring our lives to fruition.

Traditional Christian theology calls this faith-response by two names: justification by grace through faith, and sanctification. We do not have to become good enough for God to work in us; we simply respond to his gift of himself and we are enabled to live more fruitfully. What we are saying here is at least near to these traditional emphases: God has endowed us with the capacity to respond both to his creation of our original selves and to his continued working in and through us to bring that creation to its fulfillment. *But*—we must respond! And that is where choice enters the process, which we will discuss shortly.

The third assumption on which we are operating is: *We are imperfect reflections of Ultimate Creative Strength.* We are created in *the image of God* but we are not perfect exemplifications of who God is. In Bi/Polar terms, we are *out of balance* in terms of our polar strengths. Or, we are lopsided, and that creates both problems and possibilities.

The fourth assumption follows from the third: *We are tempted to pretend to be what we are not.* This is one way of looking at the story of Adam and Eve in Genesis 3:1–6. They wanted to *be* gods rather than to actualize the image of God within them. Or as Paul put it, those who know God but do not honor him for who he is (Creator) "exchanged the truth about God for a lie and worshiped and served the creature rather than the Creator . . ." (Romans 1:25).

This temptation affects us in different ways. Strongly independent persons are tempted to think they can do all things themselves—to be self-made persons. Strongly dependent persons are tempted to believe that they can negotiate life only by depending on other people. Those higher in Practical Thinking are tempted to believe that all they need is to continue dealing realistically with life without drawing on new ideas, while those stronger in Theoretical Thinking are conversely tempted to believe that if they can just think of enough ideas all will be well. Thinkers are tempted to believe they can think their way through life without risking, while Riskers are tempted to feel they can risk without thinking.

A fifth assumption is the opposite of the fourth: *We are tempted not to use all our strengths in the negotiation of life.* It is natural for the thinker to think but not do much risking—no choice is necessary to follow this natural inclination. And it is natural for the risker to risk and not do much thinking. To overcome this temptation, which is the result of our lopsidedness, we must *choose* to use all our strengths in relation to one another.

The sixth assumption is therefore: *We can choose to actualize our full potential by using all our strengths con-*

structively. Growth is not automatic, but it *is* natural. We were born to actualize our potential, but because of both inner and outer forces, we must struggle to do so. Sometimes it is the environment which holds us down, and at other times it is simply our failure to take part in the struggle.

We are not dealing *directly* with the environment in this book. To choose to use our strengths to the fullest does have an influence on the environment, however, and even when there are limiting factors which we cannot control, we can change our attitude toward them. Refusing to allow a limiting environment to dictate his style of life, Abraham Lincoln rose to become President. Susan B. Anthony used her strengths to carry forward the movement to eliminate restrictions on voting by women. Jane Addams gave her life's energies to help create a better environment for others through Hull House. Martin Luther King, Jr., used his charismatic leadership to challenge segregated buses in Montgomery, Alabama, and thereby began a move which changed the environment of blacks in the United States.

Our direct concern in this book, however, is not with reforming society but with changing people. The focus is on learning to use our strengths in interaction for both personal growth and improved relationships. The enemies of this process with which we are concerned are those within us.

One of these enemies is the overuse of our greatest strength. My practical friend whom I described in an earlier chapter is tempted to hold on to his practical routines rather than to try out new ways of doing his work. My temptation, on the other hand, is either to fall in love with ideas and to resent those who challenge them, or to move from one idea to another and not give any of them a chance to prove themselves in practice. The person whose greatest strength is Dependent Risking is tempted to become overdependent, and those with great Independent

Risking strength are tempted to hold on to their self-confidence and the power it produces and fail to depend on others for the help they need.

The other enemy is our failure to use our lesser strengths fully. Practical people may fail to use their theoretical strength, and theoretical people often do not make full use of their practical strength. Similarly, dependent people do not exercise sufficient independence and independent ones are afraid to be dependent.

Realizing our full potential means using all our strength in interaction, a process that will be delineated in detail in Chapter 7.

The seventh and final assumption is: *We grow by using our strengths, not by trying to overcome weaknesses.*

When we begin with our weaknesses, it is easy for us to become so obsessed with our problems that we lose all desire to overcome them. A few years ago I discovered how true this is with regard to grief. Our only son died of cancer at the age of twenty-one, and my world seemed to tumble in around me so that I could see no way out. Trying to overcome my grief simply turned me inward and led to further grief. It so happened that I had to begin an intensive two-weeks' teaching experience eight days after his death. There was no way out of the responsibility, for two colleagues who might have taken over were both on leave. Out of necessity I plunged into the enterprise, wondering if I could make it. My grief did not go away, but by doing what I could do well, I was gradually able to begin dealing with it.

Alcoholics Anonymous uses a similar approach. They not only come together to draw help from one another and from God; they also move ahead one day at a time. No one is asked to vow never to drink again; rather, they are asked to affirm what they can do: to go *this day* without a drink.

When I have trouble falling asleep, I find I must practice this same principle. If I begin to say, "I've got to overcome my weakness of not being able to sleep," I may lie awake for hours. But if I say, "I don't have to go to sleep; all I must do now is to enjoy the rest which being in bed brings me," then I find that sleep usually comes.

Two things can happen when we lead from strengths. We may inspire others to join with us and contribute their strength to supplement ours. Or we can learn—and it *is* a process of learning—how to use our lesser strengths in relation to our greater ones.

This is an exciting process, and I invite you to join me in learning it in the chapter that follows.

Discussion and Activity Guide

1. What are the four "life forces" which the Bi/Polar System recognizes?

2. With which one of these "life forces" does Bi/Polar deal directly?

3. What is the Bi/Polar understanding of how we are most likely to grow as a person?

4. What is *your* greatest obstacle to growth?

If you read Chapter 7 from the first page to the last, you may find it long and tedious. A plan for reading this chapter is therefore appropriate provided you feel reasonably clear about your own pattern of strengths.

1. Read the material down to the place where the growth plans for the eight patterns begin.

2. Go directly to your own pattern. Read and study its plan for growth. If you are still not sure of a pattern for yourself, try out any one that you believe might be yours, and then go on to others that are possibilities.

3. Read the other pattern plans for growth as a help in understanding how other people develop their personalities.

4. Read the concluding comments which are a transition to Chapter 8.

–7–

A Plan for Growth

When I was first introduced to the Bi/Polar System, I was quite skeptical about its potential for helping me change. Frankly, I became involved in it primarily because one of my colleagues needed an additional instructor for the growth seminars and I find it difficult to say "no" for fear of offending people. I am also interested in new ideas, and I sensed that here was something that could be provocative and challenging.

I quickly became intrigued by the insights which the Bi/Polar plan provided me concerning both myself and others. Vague hunches began to take on the character of firm understandings. I understood why all my early efforts in our marriage to make my wife over into a docile homemaker had not worked. She was far too dynamic and enterprising not to express herself on a broader scale. I also found an explanation concerning how I work with my two closest colleagues. I am the idea person; one colleague is the mover; and the other is the reconciler. "Ah ha's!" began to occur frequently as I applied my new insights to all kinds of people, and I began more systematically to alter my approach to them in terms of who they are.

I am not sure that I expected to change, but I began to
do so almost in spite of myself. Change is often painful,
especially when it means giving up familiar patterns of behavior for as yet untried ones. Bruce Larson is right, I believe, when he observes that "Most of us have an inborn
fear of change because we think it will cause us to lose
something." [1] He tells of an incident in which he and
several hundred other people were asked to pair off and
closely observe one another. Then they were told to make
some change in their appearance and observe one another
again. The interesting fact is that almost everyone in the
room took something off—glasses, watches, shoes, and so
on—rather than adding something.

By beginning with your strengths rather than weaknesses, the Bi/Polar approach to growth *adds* something
before it takes anything away. That is, you use a greater
strength to deal with a problem caused by a lesser one.
Almost before you realize what is happening, you are dealing with the problem constructively and what you have
gained is much better than what you have lost.

I do not mean to imply that all my problems have dis-
appeared. Old habits of self-negation, of letting resentment
build up until I explode, of feeling sorry for myself because I do not receive the recognition I want—these and
other typical negative behaviors of those with Patterns
One and Three strengths keep surfacing, sometimes un-
expectedly. There are times when I still find it difficult
to accept myself as I am, and again I rebel against my
God-given individuality. Why could I not have been made
as an independent, dynamic person who can slay dragons
and win battles with bold, decisive strokes of valor?

We all must fight our battles over and over again, and
I make these personal confessions for two reasons. I do
not want to create the illusion that growth is either automatic or always easy. Nor do I want you to become dis-

[1] Bruce Larson, *The One and Only You*, (Word Book Publishers, Waco, Texas, 1974, 1976) p. 32.

couraged if you find yourself slipping backward just when you think you have moved ahead. The rewards are potentially too great for you to make one or even a few tries, and then quit in defeat. As one woman put it: "I have forced myself to step out alone and change my life style. It has been painful, but good. And it's only beginning. Life is opening up in a very real way due to my awareness of Bi/Polar."

And so in this chapter I will first delineate the growth process in a general way, briefly but concretely. Illustrations in this section may or may not fit your situation. In the longer consideration of this process, I will take each of the eight patterns and with greater specificity indicate how persons with those patterns of strengths can learn to cope with life.

The four movements of the process are *achieving insight, being motivated, understanding the nature of the change process,* and *developing skills for changing.*

Achieving Insight

The insights are those that grow out of understanding the basic character of each of the eight patterns, with the variations provided by the three blends for each. (This insight was the emphasis of Chapter 5.) Nor is it just an intellectual understanding that involves acquiring information; it is also affirmation, or the internalizing of information. That is, we must affirm and accept ourselves, and we must also affirm and accept others for who they are.

One person put it this way:

> My first positive experience has been the joy of identifying and affirming a lot of beautiful strengths which I have and seeing that I'm OK. My strengths are just as important as those of anyone else. It has been enlightening and encouraging to discover that my lesser strengths are, in reality, strengths and not weaknesses.

And another said:

> One of my business associates, a Pattern Five, is sensitive
> and requires a lot of stroking, which I wasn't doing enough
> of. Now as he accomplishes things, I give him deserved
> "pats" on the back.

Self-affirmation and the affirming of others is the first
movement in the growth process.

Being Motivated

Motivation is the force from within us or from the
outside that causes us to think, feel, or act. My head hurts,
and I take an aspirin. I am dissatisfied with my present
religious beliefs, and I start thinking how I can acquire a
better set. Someone tells me about a misfortune that has
befallen a friend, and I feel sympathy and go to see
him/her to see what I can do. I see a tantalizing food ad-
vertisement on television, and I feel hungry and go to
the refrigerator.

Many motivators are much more complex, of course.
Often several factors work together to encourage change.
I am *discouraged* because of my low self-image; I am *encouraged* by Bi/Polar to have greater self-esteem; and the
two factors (pain and encouragement) work together to
make me want to do something. I recognize my tendency
to want privacy and my temptation to withdraw from involvement; I am offered a way of dealing with my pain; and
I accept and act on the proposal. Reading a book such as
this one provides me with an image of the person I might
be, and I begin steps toward actualizing the new image.

Motivations also differ in their character. Rewards and
punishment are two of the most common. Some behavioristic psychologists use both; others, such as B. F.
Skinner, use rewards primarily in a process he calls "op-
erant conditioning." A challenge, the expectations that
others have of us, our hope of becoming a more adequate
person, the example of another person are other types of

motivators. The desire to fulfill God's expectations is also a powerful motivation for many people. They ask, "What is the will of God for me in this situation?" and move toward fulfilling that expectation.

Sources of motivation are, therefore, partly from inside us: pain, ambition, thinking, feelings, guilt, for example— and partly from the outside: a book, a sermon, a new idea, other people, for example. For the religious person, a relationship with God is the ultimate motivation, though there are many "outward signs" by which this relationship is mediated.

All of these motivators operate in relation to the Bi/ Polar System. Three are the most common, however. The one most often mentioned in the case studies which I am using is a new feeling of self-esteem. Over and over again the respondents say that the idea that all arrangements of strengths are good gave them a reason for changing.

One person put it this way: I can change "because I am now more comfortable with myself and in my relationships." Another who found an increased self-respect as a motivator wrote: "I have always been intimidated by aggressive, forceful people . . . . The idea that all eight patterns are equal in worth came to me with great relief and comfort . . . . I recognize that I must affirm my own identity and grow, not change my individuality." And a third said: "I now know that in order to grow, I must step out in faith—faith in being myself at all times and not restricting my individuality."

Other people begin to acknowledge the pain that the misuse of their strengths has caused them. In an earlier chapter I told the story of a man whose failure to use his Practical Thinking strength made him unaware when he came to a Bi/Polar seminar how much his bank account was overdrawn. This pain caused him to listen to what was being said about the possibility of using our greater strengths to activate our lesser ones, and he has begun to act more practically. In another case, the pain came from speaking extemporaneously in a group and then feeling rejected when his ideas, not well articulated, were not accepted. This person's growth has taken the form of being better prepared to make his influence felt in the groups to which he belongs. In another case pain has often resulted in a young woman's acting impulsively, which is her natural response. Having felt pain many times after she has acted too quickly, she is now trying to use her Practical Thinking strength to make her more aware of all the factors involved in a situation in order to modify her impulsiveness.

A third motivation which is often activated by Bi/Polar is the desire to succeed. In one instance, an executive whose temptation is to fail to delegate authority has come to see that he cannot do everything himself and he has therefore been willing to ask for the help of others. His ability to do his job, he has come to see, is absolutely dependent on his willingness to act in this manner. In another case, an ambitious teacher whose temptation has been to withdraw from involvement with other people has come to see that his success in his profession is dependent on his willingness to relate to them.

Awareness is a key word in activating motivations to change. They are already present, for there is that quality of human nature that drives us forward. Even when we fear change, the impulse toward a better expression of who we are is present. When the circumstances of life have thwarted our self-development or when we have become protective of what small degree of self-worth we have developed, the impulse to move ahead must be awakened. We often need an outer stimulus to make us aware of the possibility of change, and the insight that comes from knowing our identity is the key which unlocks the door to our hidden potentialities.

Insight is not enough, however, nor is the motivation which arises from it necessarily sufficient to instigate change. There must also be an understanding of the process of growth, and so we now turn to this third step in our plan.

Understanding the Process

Insight about ourselves and others is the first step in the plan. The second is to become aware of the motivations which already exist within us and to begin to act as a result of them. The third phase is to understand how growth occurs.

We have already considered parts of this process in Chapters 2, 3, and 4. Some of this section will be a summary of how we use our strengths in relation to one another. This is called the "feeding process" in the Bi/Polar System.

1. *Remember the difference in a polarized and a bi/polar use of your strengths.*

Polarization means that we use one strength to the exclusion of its bi/polar opposite. That is, we use Bi/Polar Thinking *or* Bi/Polar Risking. We become fixated on Practical Thinking to the exclusion of Theoretical Thinking, or on Theoretical Thinking without using Practical Thinking. We use either Dependent or Independent Risking, but not both.

On the other hand, the bi/polar use of strengths consists of using each strength in relation to its polar opposite, and all strengths in relation to one another.

2. *Invest the fruit of one strength in its polar opposite.*

The natural activity involved in Practical Thinking is to view human situations with realism, to see things as they are. The fruit of this kind of thinking consists of facts, data, and an understanding of problems. To invest these fruits in Theoretical Thinking means that facts are used as the material to build ideas.

Theoretical Thinking results in the generation of ideas

and the ability to see things as they might be. Investing these fruits in Practical Thinking means that we use ideas as the tools to solve practical problems.

The activity of Dependent Risking leads to confidence in others, and we use our relationships with others to take more independent risks. Independent Risking results in self-confidence. Self-confidence is then used as the basis for depending more on others. That is, other people help the dependent risker gain more independence, and self-confidence is the basis for the independent risker to be able to gain strength from others.

The fruit of Bi/Polar Thinking is a combination of facts and ideas, or creative perception. These facts and ideas used in relation to one another then become the content of Bi/Polar Risking and make that Risking more creative. We invest our thinking in action.

Bi/Polar Risking leads to confidence in self and others. This creative confidence (or interdependence) makes it possible for us not only to think more creatively ourselves but also to be willing to draw facts and ideas from others. This kind of thinking, in turn, makes our action more creative.

3. *Use all your strengths in relation to one another.*

In dealing with human situations—problems, relationships, our daily existence—we usually begin with one of our greater strengths. Dependent/theoretical persons, for example, usually (though not always) begin with either Dependent Risking or Theoretical Thinking and then cross over to the polar opposite of the strength with which they begin. If, let us say, it is Theoretical Thinking, the first crossover is to Practical Thinking. Having developed more creative Thinking, the person then moves toward one of the Risking poles and engages in the same process.

Since we will be describing this process for each of the eight patterns, this one example must suffice for the present.

4. *Our tendency to think and risk in a way that is natural because of our greater strengths may lead to an undisciplined expression of that strength. That is, a tendency may become a temptation.*

Practical thinkers, for example, have a natural *tendency* to value facts, and this is good. Their *temptation* is toward an undisciplined expression of their concern for facts so that they consider facts more important than ideas. The *tendency* of theoretical thinkers is to value ideas; an *undisciplined expression* of this tendency makes them unconcerned about the use of ideas in solving problems.

The *tendency* of dependent riskers is to value the opinions and good will of others; their *temptation* is to express the tendency so strongly that they are afraid to state their own ideas, opinions, and values. The *tendency* of independent riskers is to enjoy their self-confidence; the *undisciplined expression* of the tendency leads to their unwillingness to depend on or even be concerned with others.

5. *Our temptation is to become polarized on our greater strengths and to fail to use our lesser ones.*

Our problem is not just the *over*use of our greater strengths but also the *under*use of our lesser ones. One of my greatest temptations is to think so long that I do not make a decision or act. That is, I become polarized on Thinking and my undisciplined expression of what is good keeps me from using my Risking strengths. Dr. Thomas's undisciplined expression of Theoretical Thinking leads him to fall in love with his ideas and may even keep him from putting himself in a position where they will be challenged. My practical friend is tempted to value his routines so much that he resents a challenge by new ideas, and he is therefore prevented from developing his Theoretical Thinking.

The undisciplined expression of Dependent Risking strength may lead people to be tempted to become overdependent and to fail to develop their Independent Risking strength. And the temptation of those with strong Independent Risking strength is not to utilize the contributions of others and thereby fail to develop their Dependent Risking strength.

6. *What we need, therefore, is a plan for and the skills to use all our strengths in interaction with one another.* This statement moves us to the fourth part of the growth plan.

Developing Skills

A skill is the ability to cope with a problematical situation or accomplish a particular task. It is at this point that self-help systems most often falter.

And no wonder! It is much easier to talk about insight, motivation, and understanding than to provide skills for coping with life. There are several reasons why this is true. One is that each person must negotiate his/her own plan, and thus any general plan is artificial and seems wooden. All that such a plan can do is to suggest a process which each of us must appropriate for our own use.

A second reason runs even deeper: acquiring skills is often a painful process, for it requires changes in thinking, feeling, and behaving. I have already said that change is difficult unless the motivation is strong. Most of us, at least if we are past young adulthood, are fairly fixed in our life styles. Even young people are already sufficiently established in their ways of reacting to life so that it is usually easier to go on in familiar ways of doing things.

A third reason follows from the second: many people, both young and old, need individual or group counseling as a way of uprooting the old and familiar and establishing the new and untried. This book cannot—and I think no book can—take the place of the support which comes from participating in a counseling relationship or small group. For this reason, I will suggest later in this chapter, and repeat the proposal in the final chapter, that you form for yourself such a support group of one or several additional people as you seek to follow the growth plan of this and the following chapter.

Although it is well nigh impossible to package a set of skills that everyone can use, we do know the components of such a growth plan. The first three parts—insight, motivation, and understanding—are basic. For this fourth part of the plan—acquiring skills—we can do two principal things. We can outline the steps, and we can illustrate how actual people have used the plan. The outline follows, and the illustrations are a part of the suggestions for each of the eight patterns.

1. *Understand your pattern of strengths.* This leads to insight, and insight involves an awareness of where you find it both easy and difficult to live creatively. At this point, you may need to review what was said about your pattern of strengths in Chapter 5. At the end of that chapter there are also brief comments about the three blends for the eight patterns.

2. *Decide to do something about your life.* This decision is based on motivation. One trouble with most New Year's resolutions is that those who make them are usually not motivated to keep them. A simple desire to do better is not enough. Alcoholics must often hit rock bottom before they are sufficiently motivated to seek help—that is, their pain becomes despair before they seek help. Alcoholism is a disease, however, and there are many problem areas of our lives that do not have that strong a hold on us. We usually have at least enough motivation—pain, ambition, hope, religious commitment, or some other—to deal with one problem. Alcoholics Anonymous wisely counsels its members to take one day at a time. So must the rest of us be willing to face one problem first, and then another.

3. *Identify a problem.* In this part of the plan, you are likely to begin first with a general problematical situation. "I need to lose weight." "I ought to be more friendly." "I've got to stand on my own two feet." "I must stop being so aggressive."

If you stop with such general statements, there is little or no hope for change. Out of your problem area, choose *a* problem that is manageable. "I need a diet that I can follow, and will look for one." "My relationship with Mary has not been good, and I will work on it." "My main problem is that I am careless with money." "I will concentrate on the relationship with my spouse and find ways of dealing with my aggressiveness."

4. *List the strengths and resources you have for dealing with the problem.* By "'strengths," I mean the six strengths of the three polar pairs. "Resources" are of two kinds. First, there are those growing out of your strengths—those qualities for each pattern listed in Chapter 5. Second, "resources" also include other kinds of assets—motivation, your faith-commitment, church or synagogue worship, your previous experience, other people, a supportive family and/or other small group, and so on. It is a matter of "counting your blessings," and naming them "one by one."

5. *List negative forces which will discourage you in dealing with your problem.* These are of three kinds: first, your lesser strengths (the three polar opposites of your major strengths). These cause your personality to be slanted in a way that makes some things difficult for you. Second, your greater and lesser strengths means that you have a *tendency* to act in certain ways, and this is good. But these tendencies lead to the *temptation* of an undisciplined expression—to the overuse, misuse, or underuse of your strengths. For example, it is natural for practical people to deal with facts; their temptation is to deny the usefulness of ideas. It is natural for dependent persons to relate easily to other people; their temptation is to

become overdependent.[2] Third, there are a host of other forces both within yourself and in your environment that hinder you in your growth: habits, the negative influence of others, a physical ailment, a discouraging environment, an uninteresting job, and so on. Some of these influences can be replaced, but you must learn to live with others. Your plan of growth has to take both kinds of forces into account.

6. *Decide what you can do next* (that is, *set a goal*). "My goal is to find a diet that I will be able to follow and still do my work." "My goal is to reestablish the good relationship I once had with Mary." "I will follow a plan for one week that involves using my money more wisely." "My goal is to be less aggressive in criticizing my spouse."

Your goal, especially at first, should be one that is fairly easy to attain. If your least strength is Practical Thinking, you may need to consult with a more practical person before selecting a goal. If it is not accomplishable, you will become discouraged. "One step at a time"—you cannot climb a mountain any other way.

7. *Work out a strategy for reaching your goal.* "I will make an appointment with my doctor and ask him for a suitable diet." "I will call up Mary and invite her to lunch next week." "I will make an appointment with a financial counselor to work out a budget." "I will work out a signal for my spouse to use when I begin criticizing, and use the plan initially for two weeks."

It does not matter greatly where you begin with the six strengths in carrying out your plan and your strategy so long as you use all of them. You will need some ideas (Theoretical Thinking), a plan (Practical Thinking), response and/or help from others (Dependent Risking), and a move toward carrying out the strategy (Independent Risking). And these four operating together constitute a blend of Bi/Polar Thinking and Bi/Polar Risking.

---

[2] Tendencies and temptations for each of the strengths are listed in the Appendix.

8. *Do it!*
9. *Evaluate what has happened and set another goal.*
If you reached your goal, try to understand why. If you did not, ask yourself first whether it was a realistic one. If you decide it was, why did you not reach it? What can you do next time to improve your strategy?
10. *Form your own Bi/Polar group.* We have said that one of the problems in following a book is that you have no support person or community built into the process. It will help considerably if you have one or more persons who are also working at the plan. We will have more to say on this in the final chapter.

As you grow more familiar with this process, it will become habitual and perhaps replace some of the "sloppy" ways you now follow. One person will need to write out his plan; another will carry it in his head: Some may even want to record it on a cassette tape recorder. One thing is sure: The *plan* will not work unless *you* work at it!

What follows is an analysis of how the eight patterns can learn to cope with life more constructively, and examples of how people have used the Bi/Polar plan.

PATTERN ONE [3]

Those with Pattern One strengths are almost literally the people who hold the world together. Without their stability, realism, cooperativeness, and dependability, the ordering of a democratic society would disappear into either chaos or dictatorship. More dynamic Sevens and Eights bring about change in the social order; Ones provide the cement that holds it together. No wonder that our statistics, incomplete as they are, indicate that there are more Ones than any other pattern. They are needed in great number to provide order for life.

[3] For additional data about the patterns, including major strengths, see Chapter 5.

On the other hand, these valuable persons probably feel more pain in being who they are than those of any other pattern (though Pattern Threes are similar). This is especially true in a highly competitive society where the greatest value is often placed on the dynamic person. Partly because of this cultural reality and partly because of the nature of Pattern Ones, they frequently have low self-esteem and think negatively about themselves.

It is for this reason that the Bi/Polar message that all patterns are of equal worth comes as such encouragement to Pattern Ones. As one person, a clergyman, put it: "The gospel of equal worth for persons of all eight patterns, and of growth within the pattern where one finds himself, needs to be proclaimed."

WS found his stimulus for growth in this recognition that the eight patterns of strengths are of equal worth. He had always been intimidated by aggressive, forceful people because he felt that they were superior to him. As he thought about his situation (using Practical Thinking), he began to see possibilities for a different kind of behavior (Theoretical Thinking). This was based partly on his new image of aggressive people, that they often want others to be more forceful. He also recognized that his temptation had been to let resentments build up inside, then explode, and he had withdrawn from relationships when things did not go well.

He has begun to use Dependent Risking in two ways: he commends people rather than criticizing them, and he deliberately relates more deeply with those around whom he feels comfortable. In these ways his Independent Risking strength has increased so that he can accomplish his goal of being able to deal constructively with the aggressive people whom he had both admired and feared.

WS also illustrates another common temptation of Pattern Ones—to allow the needs of others to rule their lives. Pattern Ones are also often perplexed by new situations, especially when seemingly insurmountable problems confront them. Because of the temptation to cling to established procedures, such situations can be overwhelming.

JW (see pages 28, 39, 170) went to a new job that he had been led to believe would offer relatively few problems. What he found during his first few weeks of analyzing the situation (using his Practical Thinking) was diametrically opposite to his expectations: an unorganized, demoralized, and fractioned situation that led him to despair.

He turned from his analysis of the problem to Dependent Risking and went for help from the people who had convinced him to take the position. They were embarrassed over their lack of realism about the situation and each one in turn managed to change the subject to a more pleasant topic.

JW's temptations were to withdraw from the situation, to believe that he could no nothing to change it, and to feel sorry for himself. But his future depended on his being able to meet the problems, nor was he keen on moving his family again. So, he then turned to Theoretical Thinking and began to ask, "What are the possibilities in the situation?" Not satisfied with his own perceptions, he consulted printed resources. Since people had failed him, perhaps he could find help elsewhere, he reasoned. Through an interplay between Practical and Theoretical Thinking, he began to devise plans for dealing with the most pressing problems.

Using the encouragement of his wife and a few close friends (Dependent Risking), he began to move out through Independent Risking. He set for himself first one goal and then another, and turned to dealing with them in terms of strategies based on the best thought he could devise. As he began to move ahead, seeming much more dynamic than he knows himself to be, he accomplished one goal after another. His friends who had failed to give him aid are now high in their praise of what he has done, and he has thus grown from a condition that could have led to overdependency to one in which his self-confidence has greatly increased.

JW illustrates how easily Pattern Ones can develop overdependency in relationships. Being forced to become self-reliant when friends failed him caused him to use both his Theoretical Thinking and Independent Risking more fully than had been his custom. His case also indicates, as does the one following, that the key to growth in Pattern Ones is careful planning prior to action. Their Practical Thinking strength makes this feasible, but they often need encouragement from others and their ideas to activate their Theoretical Thinking.

BW's problem was how to convince the school principal that the PTA program needed a new format. She began with her Practical Thinking as the basis of recognizing deficiencies in the previous programing. She then utilized her Theoretical Thinking by imagining what might be substituted, and she consulted with others (thus using Dependent Risking) for additional suggestions and for help in formulating her plan. She had done her homework thoroughly before asking for an appointment with the principal.

Using her Independent Risking strength and armed with the results of the use of her other three strengths, she went to the principal, presented her plan, answered the objections she had anticipated that he would raise, and maintained good communication with him throughout the conference. He approved the changes and they were later implemented.

All of these Pattern Ones operated out of their major strength, which caused them to be realistic. WS then became a theoretical One and having made his plan became on some occasions a Warm One and on others an Assertive One. JW, normally relationally oriented and thus a Warm One, was forced by circumstances to become a Theoretical One, and then an Assertive One. BW was both a Realistic, Theoretical, and Warm One as she developed her plan and eventually became an Assertive One as she presented the plan to the principal.[4]

In most instances the clue to the growth of Pattern Ones is their use of their strengths for the careful formulation of plans. The order is often: analysis of the problem (Practical Thinking), ideas for change (Theoretical Thinking), checking with others or asking for their help (Dependent Risking), and putting the plan into operation (Independent Risking). As these strengths operate together they are using a blend of Bi/Polar Thinking and Bi/Polar Risking.

BW illustrates a common need of Pattern Ones: they must "borrow trouble" by anticipating the problems that may arise. Their Independent Risking is usually not great enough, especially as they begin a plan of growth, for them to "play it by ear" as they move into action.

Pattern Two

When others vacillate, Pattern Twos hold steady; when others permit disorder, Twos help to restore discipline; when others are rocking the boat, the Two will be at the

---

[4] For additional information on pattern blends, see Chapter 5.

helm, keeping a steady course ahead, even in uncharted waters. If you want something done well and want to be sure that all details are worked through, ask a Pattern Two! These qualities grow out of the Practical/Independent combination in Pattern Twos. We can depend on them to be realistic, well-organized, disciplined, serious, self-sufficient, consistent, and tenacious. We should not even be surprised if at times they are direct to the point of being blunt. These characteristics are absolutely necessary in situations that require a controlling voice without fear or favor. Twos may have problems in situations where they cannot easily exercise authority, and they need to learn how to work more constructively with others. Their contribution to life can be measurably lessened unless this occurs.

Their least strength is Dependent Risking, and their tendency toward self-sufficiency can lead to the undisciplined expression of Independent Risking. Their tendency toward consistency and to evaluate the new before accepting it may also lead to the temptation to resist change.

The temptation to resist change is overcome as they use their Theoretical Thinking strength and become idealistic Twos. They can act more decisively and become assertive Twos as they use their Independent Risking not only in the realm of ideas but also in the area of doing. They can become warm Twos as they accept their own pattern of strengths, affirm their identity, and thereby become more open in their relationships. Until this occurs, they often mistakenly identify silence with Christian charity and make it difficult for their associates to relate to them in their withdrawn condition.

ST had been an enigma for those with whom he worked. They greatly respected his abilities and solicited his point of view, but he often did not express it and would withdraw into himself even when he was with other people.

The result of his Bi/Polar inventory, placing
him in the Pattern Two arrangement of strengths,
came as a great shock. He was a committed
Christian, and Christians (he thought) are always
supposed to be highly relational. He had felt
guilty all his life for not finding it easy to relate to
people, and here was confirmation that people
really saw him as lacking such ability. His way of
disagreeing had been to exercise what he interpreted as Christian restraint, and remain silent.
The only problem was that he was usually confident of his position, and he often ignored what
others said or decided. He was well on the way
to becoming a "decayed" Two—one who wanted
to control but had fewer and fewer people whom
he could influence.

Later, he observed that he had, after a long
period of thought, decided he might as well be
himself even though he saw his natural self as
undesirable. But then a strange thing happened
as he began to affirm his strengths and be more
open in his relationships with others. He had
analyzed and diagnosed his situation, using
Practical and Theoretical Thinking and then began to use his Independent Risking more fully
by speaking out when he had previously remained silent.

This meant that his associates found it much
easier to relate to him because of his new openness. They still might not agree, but they knew
where he stood. And as these associates in turn
opened up to him more fully and expressed their
appreciation of him, his least strength, Dependent Risking, began to grow. Instead of being
less acceptable, as he had feared, he has found
more acceptance, and he therefore has a more
creative relationship with others.

The growth pattern of Twos follows that of Ones in that
both usually begin with their two Thinking strengths to-

gether. The next move for Pattern Twos is quite different, however; they must use their Independent Risking as a means of developing better relationships. The temptation of Twos not to put themselves in a dependent relationship is overcome by their remaining true to their convictions but in a more open manner. When this occurs, other people are more likely to listen to what they have to say.

RC (see page 73) is a businessman whose relationships with his colleagues has always been minimal. He did his job well, and the inner circle to which he belonged in his business had learned to depend on him always to be efficient and effective in his work.

He has recently come to realize that his lack of relational concern has hindered him in his work. His original growth goal was to speak up in the weekly meeting of his associates when he had something to say rather than withdrawing into himself. On his first attempt, he planned carefully what to say and how to communicate his proposal. To do this he used both poles of his Thinking strength, and then moved to Independent Risking in order to relate to his associates, thus also using his Dependent Risking. He has found that not only do others listen to what he has to say but also that his recommendations are often followed. And his general relationships with his colleagues have improved in the process.

Twos are also tempted not to express their feelings but rather to be objective and thus to appear totally uncompromising. What they often discover is that when they do express their feelings, they can become more effective in their work.

KV (see page 74) is a church business manager, a fairly Warm Two in that he relates more easily to others than many Pattern Twos. He keeps a controlled watch on the church budget, however, especially on expenditures by staff members. They often feel that he is unresponsive to their program needs.

After he had thought through his situation, using Practical and Theoretical Thinking, he began to use Independent Risking to let his fellow staff members know the kind of data he wants before he grants their budget requests. "Have your facts in hand," he said, "and don't back down when I raise questions. Argue with me, but be sure you have your needs clearly defined, and know the reasons for them. You might be surprised at what I will do." This new openness on his part has helped his colleagues in knowing how to relate to KV in business matters, and in turn his overall relationship with them has improved.

Since Pattern Twos do not usually speak with ease, their first step in growth is usually the use of their Thinking strengths both to analyze the situation, to consider other possibilities, and to formulate a plan. Having done so, they are able to move toward Independent Risking which puts them in relationship with others. As they practice more openness in their own disciplined manner, their Dependent Risking strength is fed and their relationships improve.

One of the basic needs of the Pattern Two is to accept the wisdom of the AA prayer, and thus to realize there are some things they can control, and some things they cannot, and to try to distinguish between the two. This is especially important when they are in a situation where they cannot maintain complete control. Their gifts will always be needed, however, and they can seek out those tasks which particularly demand them. As they relax more in their relationships, they will find themselves being listened to and able to exercise greater influence without the control which many people resent.

PATTERN THREE

Pattern Threes have many characteristics in common with Ones. Their differences grow out of the fact that Three's greatest strength is Theoretical Thinking, and their major contribution to life is the ability to assimilate and be able to dispense a large repertoire of ideas. Their ideas are usually not original; in a sense they are "collectors of ideas," often serving as a reconciler between opposing points of view. Their natural tendency is to look for truth wherever it may be found rather than to support a single point of view, and then to see these different perspectives in relation to one another.

They have a kind of orderliness about them, but it is likely to be in the realm of the theoretical rather than the practical—Ones often have a neatly arranged office, Threes are much less likely to do so. They tend to be quiet, but articulate when they feel confident; to be considerate of others, introspective, and often shy. They are not only sensitive to the needs of others but also sensitive with regard to the way others treat them. They are often vulnerable to the hurts of others but are more likely to bear their own hurt in silence than to articulate it.

Because their least strength is Independent Risking and their greatest is Theoretical Thinking, their major temptation is to *live in the world of ideas* rather than to act on the basis of their ideas. They often continue speculating when they should be doing, even to the point of neglecting daily responsibilities.

LG is a university professor who enjoys planning a course more than teaching it, who had rather write out an idea than to present it orally. When he has a number of practical matters pressing to be done, he has found that the best way to get them done is to make a list and check items off the list as he does them.

His formula for coping with life is to plan carefully, moving back and forth between Theoretical and Practical Thinking, and he is more comfortable when the plan is in writing. He is sometimes able to move directly to Independent Risking, thereby operating out of the Three-Four, or Independent, blend. More often he prefers to consult with others, thus operating as a Warm Three, prior to using Independent Risking. His willingness to expose his ideas through consultation represents growth, because at one time he was reluctant to do so for fear of being rejected.

He still has problems in moving from Thinking to Risking and is tempted to become polarized on Bi/Polar Thinking. He often prefers for others to put his ideas to work, and then resents the fact that they, rather than he, receive the credit. As he has learned to plan more carefully, attending to details, he has found it possible to risk more creatively both dependently and independently in order to accomplish a task.

Pattern Threes are tempted to live on the "ragged edge" of catastrophe, preferring to think too long and to act too slowly, to keep thinking about a problem when they should be taking action. An illustration of this temptation is found in the problem that JA (see page 78 in Chapter 5) had in completing a term paper in one of my courses. He could not finish it to his satisfaction, until several months after the course ended. It is also demonstrated in the following case:

ME (see pages 48 and 76) admits to living much of her life prior to her experience with

Bi/Polar on a survival basis. Her anxiety level was high as she imagined all sorts of dire consequences in the life of her family.

Bi/Polar, as she puts it, has moved her to the self-actualization level—to a point where she has been able to take charge of her life rather than letting circumstances control her. She still depends a great deal on Theoretical Thinking to help her sort things out but is increasingly able to move to Practical Thinking through more careful planning. In one instance she began with Practical Thinking by recognizing that the church of which her husband is pastor was becoming so activity-centered that the situation was about to become chaotic. She then moved to Theoretical Thinking and came up with the idea of putting a church calendar on the wall so that church members could write in all the activities of their groups for a month's time. By this time in her pilgrimage, her Independent Risking had grown sufficiently that she simply put the calendar on the wall, but did it anonymously. The idea worked, she admitted that it was hers, and received a good response, thus growing in self-confidence and her relationships with others.

As she has continued in her growth plan, she has been more and more willing to risk her ideas and at the same time give people freedom to reject them. She has found in this process that she receives considerable affirmation of her Thinking strength, and thus as she has increased in Risking strength, her Theoretical Thinking has become more creative.

One theoretical Three, a businessman who tended to carry out his responsibilities with inadequate practicality, admits to having been long frustrated by his Pattern Two wife's practicality and overwhelmed by his Pattern Eight employer. He summarized his growth process in an especially perceptive sentence: "I'm finding my strengths are developed as I use my dependency to allow others to help me develop auxiliary strengths of practicality which boosts my confidence for becoming more independent." The process also enhances his greatest strength, Theoretical Thinking, as it is fed by a better use of his Practical Thinking for whose increase he still depends on others.

Since my own Pattern is Three, I can understand the subtle temptations which the Theoretical/Dependent person faces. My own greatest temptation is to become polarized on Thinking and not take the risk involved in acting. I find that I must plan with care if my Risking is to grow. There are times when I become a Warm Three and am tempted to become overdependent. I am more likely to be a Realistic Three, especially in relation to teaching colleagues' preoccupation with theory. I am even inclined at times to be an Independent Three, to throw caution to the wind and express my ideas dogmatically and forcefully, especially when frustrations have built up over a period of time. I then try not to worry about the consequences, but usually do. So I know basically that I ought always to plan carefully, include in my planning the projection of the action needed, and however reluctantly, move forward for the implementation of my plans.

PATTERN FOUR

Pattern Fours are unique, and if our experience in Bi/Polar seminars is typical, also few in number. History supports our inconclusive data that there are relatively few genuinely innovative people. Leonardo da Vinci, Queen Elizabeth I,[5] Benjamin Franklin, Immanuel Kant, Thomas

[5] Queen Elizabeth I could just as well have been a Pattern Eight. Because of the innovative character of her reign and the intense vitality which it generated in British life, I am inclined to think she was a Four, surrounded by others who carried out her innovative ideas.

A. Edison, and Albert Einstein are rightly considered exceptional people, and their creativity marks them as Pattern Fours. The existence of only a small number of Fours, along with the distribution of other patterns, can be understood as part of the wisdom of the Creator and as evidence for design in creation. Too many innovative people would lead to a cacophony of discordant voices far more devastating than the present diversity of the human family.

The originality of Pattern Fours is the result of a strong combination of Theoretical Thinking and Independent Risking. Their search for the new may be almost entirely in the realm of theory, as in the case of the idealistic Einstein (though with tremendous practical implications); they may be more practically bent, as in the case of the realistic Edison; they may be more action-oriented, as in the case of the assertive Queen Elizabeth; or they may be more people-oriented, as in the case of the warm Franklin.

The strongest tendency of Pattern Fours is to live in the world of ideas; their greatest temptation is to think about ideas so much that the practical is neglected. Consider how many inventions Leonardo da Vinci projected in theory and design without trying them out. Fours value their independence; they are tempted to withdraw from involvement with others and live in the world of ideas. Even extremely gifted thinkers such as Einstein must at least expose their ideas to others, and it may be their more practically-minded colleagues who will understand and put their ideas into practice.

Fours with fewer native gifts have more problems, especially if they want their innovative ideas to be accepted by others. Only by a conscious use of their two Thinking strengths together, along with Independent Risking to make them willing to expose their ideas to others and thus use their Dependent Risking, will others profit from the fruits of their Theoretical Thinking.

AL (see page 80) was able to define and accept herself only as the result of a Bi/Polar seminar. She had known that the role expectations of a pastor's wife were not satisfying but she did not understand why. She came to see that if she were going to be a whole person, she had to grow in her relationship strength. Only in this way could her innovative Thinking be known and appreciated by other people. It has not been easy for her, but she is trying, while at the same time maintaining her true Theoretical/Independent self.

J. W. Thomas, the originator of the Bi/Polar System, was not content with the small circle of influence which his ideas had so long as he was using them only in his work as a management consultant. As we noted in Chapter 2, he deliberately sought the help of a dynamic and enterprising person to help increase their influence. At about the same time, he put the ideas in book form.[6] It was his own System that led him to see the necessity of these risks. He recognized his need both for others' practicality and their action-oriented risking because of the pain he felt in not being able to achieve adequate exposure for his ideas.

He admits that his greatest difficulty has been in entrusting the writing of this book to me. Only because he has come to understand that his temptation is to be so idea-centered that others become lost in his rhetoric could he use his Independent Risking to become dependent on another person to deal with his ideas and to leave me and the publishers free in developing the book as we believe it should be.

Dr. Thomas's way of using his System for his personal life is typical of those whose greatest strength is Theoreti-

---

[6] *Your Personal Growth*, now out-of-print.

cal Thinking. This is especially the case with Pattern Fours and almost equally the case with Pattern Threes. The *intellectual understanding* precedes the *emotional risking*. As Thomas came to understand the implications of his ideas for his own life, he was able to risk more fully. The use of Independent Risking—that is, risking himself—was his way of moving toward Dependent Risking. As this has happened for him, he has been able to appreciate dependent riskers more fully.

In both AL and Dr. Thomas, the motivation for growth grew out of Practical Thinking: "I'm not a whole person"; "My ideas are not getting adequate exposure." The next point of growth was Theoretical Thinking: "Here is a new way of accomplishing my purpose." Using their Independent Risking, they moved toward others, thus having to become more dependent. Having discovered a dependable source of help, they began to grow in their Dependent Risking. In the case of Dr. Thomas, his Theoretical Thinking has continued to grow as his colleagues have questioned, challenged, disagreed. As a consequence, he has done more thinking, changed terminology, found ways of clarifying basic ideas, and chosen new procedures for conducting the Bi/Polar seminars. Throughout this process, the *basic* thrust of the system of ideas has remained intact; its *details* have been considerably improved, and its terminology and clarity of expression have changed greatly.

PATTERN FIVE

The greatest asset of Pattern Fives is warmth in relationships. They also have the strength of practicality, and the combining of the two leads them to seek out ways of implementing their concern for others. They are therefore often reconcilers in their dealing with people by seeking to bring together those out of harmony with one another. They are friendly, often assertively helpful, generous, and sensitive to the needs of others. They like to work with people, using diplomacy in doing so.

Their natural tendency is both to depend on others and to allow others to depend on them. Their temptation is to become overly dependent on others or to allow others to *use* them. Their great need often is to express themselves in relation to those who are more assertive and come to think of the Five as an "easy touch." Pattern Fives may "smother" their children by giving in too easily to the children's wishes. This undisciplined expression of a natural tendency on the part of the parent is helpful to neither parent nor child.

Because of their natural tendency to maintain good relationships, Pattern Fives may seek to avoid confrontation at all costs. They therefore may fail to express their own thoughts and feelings, a fact that means they are polarized on Dependent Risking. Because of their Practical Thinking strength, they are also often tempted to minimize or even deny the importance of new ideas and new ways of doing things.

Pattern Fives are naturally warm. They can become more assertive by deliberately expressing their Independent Risking, often depending on someone else for the courage to do so, or a situation may produce the same result. We noted in Chapter 5 that former President Gerald Ford, known in his congressional days as a "nice guy," began to be much more assertive as the demands of the presidential office called forth from him his Independent Risking strength.

Pattern Fives can also express a realistic blend by using their Thinking strengths more creatively, beginning with the practical as a means of helping them see the need for new ideas. The idealistic Five is one who quite deliberately uses his/her Theoretical Thinking strength to be at home in the realm of ideas.

PW, an example used on page 85, was forced to become more assertive as she was faced early in life with the responsibility of rearing her family alone. When she was introduced to the Bi/Polar idea, she saw herself as more independent than dependent because of this fact. What she had done was to draw upon Practical Thinking (I must support my family) to use her Theoretical Thinking to imagine career possibilities. As she entered a new career, she drew upon others (Dependent Risking) to become more assertive (Independent Risking). As these strengths operated together, she became an effective professional and because of her greater self-confidence her Risking strength became a creative combination of dependence and independence.

CW (see page 48) has become an assertive Five by developing acknowledged expertise in a field of teaching. When he was asked to begin a program of training, it was partly his Dependent Risking that made it difficult for him to refuse the invitation. His Practical Thinking made it relatively easy for him to acquire the skills necessary to carry on the program, and as he was confronted with the breadth of the field he began reading books (using his Theoretical Thinking) to become better informed. As he began to try out the program, he met with a good response (Dependent Risking) and his Independent Risking grew to the point where he now often operates as an assertive Five.

LW (see page 52) has become a more realistic Five by dealing with the fact that her husband wanted fewer relationships than she did. For many years she had chafed under his tendency to want "space." As she came to understand him in a Bi/Polar seminar, she used her Practical Thinking strength as the basis for recognizing that her expectations of him were unrealistic.

She then used her Theoretical Thinking to find ways in which she could use her Dependent Risking without involving him. She sought more relationships outside her marriage including the acceptance of responsibilities in a group to which she belonged. As she received good response from group members, her Independent Risking grew, and her relationships are actually better and her Thinking has also improved.

OW was a Pattern Five student with whom I worked closely as he pursued an advanced degree which involved a project carried out in a church. It became evident to me as we worked together that he needed encouragement in thinking through the theoretical basis for his practical work. His Dependent Risking made him willing to listen to my ideas for additional reading, which he did, and his Theoretical Thinking grew. His Dependent Risking was useful again as he developed a good relationship with the people involved in his project and with his supervisor. As he progressed through the project, the supervisor's strongest point of commendation was that he showed greater assertiveness in his leadership. He had therefore grown in two Pattern Five blends—the theoretical and the assertive.

PW began with Independent Risking strength partly because of circumstances and grew in other strengths as a consequence. CW's greater assertiveness has resulted from the self-confidence he gained in his mastery of a particular field of teaching. LW began with her Practical Thinking strength, moved to Theoretical Thinking for ideas, then used her ideas through Independent Risking, and has also grown in Dependent Risking as it has become more creative. OW began with Dependent Risking, grew in his Theoretical Thinking, worked out a practical plan based on good ideas, and grew in assertiveness. His relationship with the second group with which he worked was improved because of this additional self-confidence.

As one woman put it, "The most significant learning [in a Bi/Polar seminar] has been that I must use my natural strengths to grow the other strengths . . . . It has affirmed again my evolving awareness of myself as a woman enjoying her liberation and has given me increased confidence to express myself and make my contribution in male and female gatherings, with no feelings of apology."

PATTERN SIX

Pattern Sixes are also warm, accepting people. They like to be with people and often are "the life of the party." Usually they are emotionally expressive, talkative, and assertive in their relationships. Sixes often have developed some form of entertaining others or would like to do so, and usually they can be amusing without great effort.

The radical difference between them and Pattern Fives is that they are stronger in Theoretical Thinking. As a consequence, their imaginations are often keenly developed —they can become great tellers of stories, for example. Also, they are usually optimistic and tend to look on the bright side of things, able to imagine that things are better than they are.

These two major constellations of qualities are natural tendencies, the exercise of which brings flair to the life of others. Both tendencies are easily overused, however. Relationships with people expressed in an undisciplined fashion lead to overdependence, to the temptation of depending on other people when they should be depending on themselves. The great gift of imagination can also be misused, to the point that it becomes a substitute for reality. Dreaming can become daydreaming.

Sixes often need a person or a group to help them begin dealing with these and other temptations. Unfortunately, their dependence on the support person or group can also become overdependency. In relating to a Pattern Six, the support person or group may have to provide the outside motivation which spurs the Six to greater assertiveness and a more practical approach to life.

In the case of LT, a clergyman, it was a Bi/ Polar seminar that served as the catalyst for change. He had been a high risker, actually an assertive Six, often without using much Practical or Theoretical Thinking. His response to the seminar was as if he had been waiting for someone to say, "_____, you've got capabilities you aren't now using." As he puts it, the seminar provided the stimulus for the "Ah ha!" which suddenly made things fall in place. The new insight, which he accepted in his typical impulsive way, activated his thinking to the point where he could dare cross over the line from impulsive Risking to Creative Thinking. Before he left the seminar, he had worked with a practical, assertive leader who helped him think through what he would do when he returned home.

His first act was to call his family together and apologize to them, including his wife, for trying to make them over into people they were not. Next he put his Risking strengths to work to draw upon the strengths of others to complete a major task which he had been postponing for weeks. He also used his new-found Thinking strengths to put his finances in order (he had been close to declaring personal bankruptcy when he went to the seminar).

Shortly thereafter he went to another situation where racial strife threatened to erupt in the public schools. He was elected president of the ministerial association and used his position to work with both Protestant and Roman Catholic clergy to draw up a plan for dealing with the situation. After the committee had completed its work, he went to the leading Roman Catholic priest, whom he identified as a Pattern Two, and asked him to review the plan carefully, checking it for errors. The priest approved the plan, supported it, and the racial strife was avoided. In this process he used not only all of his own strengths but also those of other members of the local clergy.

LT's increase in Thinking strength has recently been recognized by his appointment to a position in which thinking is generally considered a prerequisite.

CM (see page 87) is also an assertive Six who had stifled her Independent Risking because of her belief that as a minister's wife she was supposed to be dependent and because of the image that her mother had of her as a "sweet little girl" who did what was expected. As it did with LT the Bi/Polar seminar provided her with the insight that she not only could be but actually was more independent than the image she had been projecting. She also began to see her need of more practicality.

Beginning with her new expression of Independent Risking and with the encouragement of her more practical husband (Dependent Risking), she has begun to express her Theoretical Thinking in more practical ways by returning to school to prepare for a career in counseling. This new image of her possibilities has been, as she puts it, exhilarating—and painful—"as growth is," she adds.

DL (see pages 48 and 52), a theoretical Six, has found it most helpful to grow in her practicality. One of her problems has been to expect too much of people, a common temptation of Pattern Sixes. With the help of several people, she has used both of her Risking strengths to overcome this temptation while at the same time using her Theoretical Thinking strength to reach toward more realistic expectations (thus becoming more practical). As she has done so, she has also grown in Independent Risking and is being more realistic about her temptation to over-dependency.

LT was already an assertive Six, polarized on his Bi/Polar Risking strength. What he needed was stimulation for both his Theoretical and Practical thinking to become both more idealistic and more realistic. This help came first from the Bi/Polar idea, and then from the seminar leader who helped him work out a plan based on good theory. CM, on the other hand, needed assurance that her assertiveness as a woman was acceptable. Her husband helped her use her Practical Thinking strength, and this in turn improved her theory. DL's first need was to become more realistic. From this growth step she has been able to begin to move toward greater assertiveness.

The naturally warm and dependent nature of the Pattern Six makes it easy for these people to listen to others who offer help. Their temptation is to become too dependent on the helper. As they persist in the growth process, however, their dependency needs will gradually decrease in proportion to the increase in their self-confidence.

One Pattern Six described his growth process in these words: "When independent action is appropriate in my life, I think my way into it. That is, I devise alternative plans (using Theoretical and Practical Thinking) and then go to several of my colleagues to check them out, help me change them, and receive support (Dependent Risking). Then having gathered support for myself and my ideas, I take the independent action (Independent Risking). This pattern has become so much a part of the way I operate now that I take it for granted. And as the habit is strengthened, Independent Risking actually becomes easier. It still costs me psychic energy, but it is easier and I feel much better about myself afterward. The payoff, in other words, is Bi/Polar growth."

PATTERN SEVEN

The gift of Pattern Sevens to humankind is their natural inclination to get things done. Without them we would have stability, ideas, and warmth in human relationships, but we might still be living in caves. The self-made American man is the typical Seven. Women have had a difficult time in finding ways of expressing their dynamic strength in our male-dominated culture, as have ethnic minorities who have not been fully accepted in the mainstream of American culture.

The outstanding characteristic of Pattern Sevens is their natural assertiveness. They provide leadership which others often gladly follow. Their individualism, self-reliance, and enterprise are coupled with realism, the result of strong Independent Risking and Practical Thinking.

As with all the other patterns, they often become polarized on their strengths and use them in an undisciplined manner. Their natural tendency is to be self-confident; their temptation is to love power for its own sake. Sevens find it easy to rely on themselves; their temptation is to fail to depend on others to complement their strengths. They have a high drive toward activity; their temptation is to be impatient with others less driven. Because they make decisions easily, this may lead to hasty and unwise choices that affect both them and others. They want facts and action, but may fail to listen to ideas and modify their actions to fit the present need.

The core character of the Seven is assertiveness which grows out of Independent Risking. When they use their Dependent Risking strength in relating to others they become Warm Sevens. They are realistic, even about themselves, when they learn to use Practical Thinking fully. They can even be idealistic as they draw upon Theoretical Thinking, their own and that of others.

JMB (see page 51) is a dynamic person who dares (using Independent Risking) to reach out to others (Dependent Risking) to increase her Thinking strength. When there is a task to accomplish, she uses her Practical Thinking to analyze carefully what the task involves and then uses her Theoretical Thinking to secure ideas from others as well as from the use of her own least strength. In a task-centered situation, she is well-organized and in control of details (a Realistic Seven). However, in relation to those with whom she is working, she also shows genuine warmth through her Dependent Risking. In this way she was able to negotiate successfully the "man's world" long before the feminist movement.

When she is dealing with ideas, she uses her Practical Thinking again to analyze the problem and then depends on other people or printed resources to enrich her Theoretical Thinking. As she uses these other strengths, her Independent Risking grows to the point where she is convincing and persuasive in her spoken presentations.

Because of the dynamic character of their personality, Sevens are often able to present an image of themselves that they believe is acceptable to those who count in their lives.

When RG, a clergyman, first asked friends to fill out his Bi/Polar inventories, all of them saw him as a Pattern Three. Only he and his wife understood his true character as a Seven. Using his Practical Thinking, he began to analyze why this was the case. He soon came to the theory, later proved, that he had been projecting a false image before his friends, most of whom were more academically oriented than he. Using his Independent Risking to "level" with friends (Dependent Risking), he admitted his "phoniness," and began to be more genuinely himself. He could then accept himself as the initiator in a group, as one who must then be willing to listen to others as they pointed out the inconsistencies and inadequacies of his ideas.

A year later when he asked friends to complete the inventory forms again, he had so changed his image that he came out consistently a Pattern Seven. He began to realize that he could not do the reading he needed to do at his church office, for he was so task-oriented that he allowed even relatively unimportant things to divert him from his studying; so he began doing his reading at home before going to his office. His preaching has improved, and his overall ministry has been enhanced as he has deliberately selected associates whose gifts complement his. He has used his Thinking strength and his Independent Risking to feed his Dependent Risking so that he is willing both to acknowledge their strengths and to use them in relation to his own.

One of the temptations of Sevens is to allow their self-confidence to subvert them into believing that no one can operate as effectively as they, and they therefore find it difficult to delegate responsibility. If this pattern continues, they will in fact lose their own effectiveness since even strong persons are limited in what they can do.

RT (see page 50) is an effective department head who before his encounter with Bi/Polar seldom allowed his secretary to assume responsibilities. As a consequence, by his own admission, he always carried in his briefcase a sheaf of unanswered letters waiting for an opportune time to answer them, a time that often arrived too late for the answer to do any good. As a consequence of this and other failures to depend on others, his work was in danger of deteriorating.

On the strength of insights from Bi/Polar, his first step was to analyze this problem, draw on a friend's Theoretical Thinking, and then use his Independent Risking to become more dependent through making his principal secretary an Administrative Assistant. It was not easy at first for him to let loose of his responsibilities, but he gradually grew in dependence on her. Eventually he turned over to her complete responsibility for one phase of his work. He was thus able to begin new enterprises, and he has recently begun to realize that he needs to use the same strategy with respect to other aspects of his work.

Coping with life, as we noted in the first part of this chapter, is not something we learn to do easily and then coast. Rather, it is often a constant struggle, as this last illustration indicates. Perhaps we will eventually establish new ways of doing things that become almost automatic, but the transfer from one aspect of life to another does not always follow. Pattern Sevens, who are naturally reluctant to ask for help, need someone who will regularly confront them with their need as they lapse into former habits that rule out a dependency relationship. An assertive Pattern One or Three is an indispensable aid for the Seven.

Pattern Eight

The Pattern Eight combination of Independent Risking and Theoretical Thinking makes these people both dynamic and imaginative. Their Risking is not only assertive; it is also abetted by the vision stemming from Theoretical Thinking. They are therefore inclined to be idealistic or idea-oriented, optimistic, enthusiastic, and irrepressible. Often we call them "charismatic personalities"—they are able to sway others either by their oratory or their personal forcefulness or both. Because they may be impetuous, they are able to promote new ideas and visions. Thereby they are stimulators of change.

Their problems, perhaps more obviously than those of other patterns, grow out of their strengths. When there are no inner or circumstantial forces at work to discipline their natural tendencies, they are tempted to overextend themselves. As they dream of more and more worlds to conquer, they reach out toward these worlds and often do conquer them only to have their empire disintegrate for lack of practical plans to hold it together. Alexander the Great of the fourth century B.C. is a typical example. Realistic enough to utilize the help of others, he nevertheless eventually overextended himself and tried to invade India only to have his troops mutiny. As concerned with bringing a unified culture to the world as conquering it, he laid the foundations on which the Roman Empire was later built and which provided the milieu in which Christianity four centuries later could begin its spread as a world religion.

With his visions and natural lack of practicality, the Pattern Eight always needs a stable person at his side, one whose realism balances his idealism. The Pattern Eight needs someone whose organizing ability complements his vision and drive.

ET (see page 96) is an unusually able student with whom I have worked closely. In one course she proposed a project to fulfill course requirements whose grand design would have required virtually full-time attention for implementation. Since she is a Warm Eight, she consulted with me about the project. I pointed out that she was about to overextend herself again and helped her design a more realistic plan. I was the catalyst to stimulate her Practical Thinking without negating her vision. She not only made her idea more workable but recognized her need of help

**from others and completed the project through
the use of all her strengths.**

The temptation of Pattern Eights, however, is to rely on
themselves to the exclusion of others. If they succeed—
and they often do—they may begin to think themselves
invulnerable. Their first growth need is often to recognize
that they too are human and must be able to trust others.

One Pattern Eight, an interior designer, realized that he
could not do his work alone; his problem was that people
never did things quite the way he wanted them done.
"They always seem to fail me," he kept saying. The only
response I knew to make was, "Well, you'd better keep
looking until you find those whom you *can* trust." I am
not sure that he heard my counsel or that he was ready to
follow it: perhaps there *was* no one who would do things
exactly as he desired.

Other Pattern Eights do learn how to use their Dependent Risking, however.

**PM responded positively to the theory of Bi/
Polar and moved from this theory to Practical
Thinking to analyze his need. He came to see
that he must set more realistic goals for himself
and temper the demands he made on both himself and others. Perhaps part of his willingness
to use the new theory was the fact that his wife
had recently divorced him and he was in serious
pain about himself.**

**Moving again from Bi/Polar theory to Practical
Thinking, he began to be clearer about what he
calls the "payoffs and pitfalls" of Dependent
Risking. As a newly single person, he recognized
the danger of an impetuous move toward a second marriage. Using both Thinking strengths, he
devised a plan that required him to reach out to
a variety of other people, thus using both his In-**

dependent and Dependent Risking. Through Risking he has moved toward others, and through Thinking he has determined *how* to do so for best results. In an interesting afterthought he adds that he has come to appreciate thinkers more but that he still prefers those who lead with feeling. His *respect* rather than his *affection* for thinkers has increased.

Prior to his Bi/Polar experience, WH had had trouble in affirming his Independent Risking strength, partly because as a clergyman he believed that the servant role required him to deny his self-confidence. As he also recognized that his greater Thinking strength was theoretical, he began to see the need for deliberately depending on others before he began to promote his ideas. He could now affirm and use his Independent strength to reach out to others to receive from them the results of their Practical Thinking to stimulate his own. As he has done so, he has found that they become more dynamic and he more stable and realistic. "It is great," he writes, "to relate to persons who are totally different in perspective and realize that we can both grow from the relationship, rather than each trying to win out over the other."

Bi/Polar insights helped WH become a more Realistic Eight as his relationships grew and he drew practical strength from others. As he realized the value of their help, he thereby became a Warm Eight. The overall result, beginning with his acceptance of his independence, has been a more creative blend of his Risking strengths and his Thinking strengths.

A trust relationship with one or a few people is difficult but essential for Pattern Eights. The trusted other must be sufficiently assertive to "nudge" Eights toward self-understanding first, and later toward drawing upon the stability strength of the other to activate their own. Pattern Eights have the potentiality of making a tremendous contribution to their life-situation; the potentiality will not be fully realized unless they have a more practical person at their side or learn to use their own Practical Thinking strength in relation to their Theoretical.

* * * * * * * *

We have now completed the presentation of the eight patterns of growth. Since people learn to cope with life in different ways, you will need to find your own variation on the suggestions made. Another person, preferably with different strengths, or a small group can be of great help in this process.

Since so many of our problems involve relationships with others, we will deal directly with improving relationships in the chapter that follows. The underlying process is essentially what we have considered in this chapter—the ten-step plan that involves insight, motivation, understanding, and skills. Much of our pain—a common motivation for change—comes out of broken or unsatisfactory relationships. It is in this area that Bi/Polar has usually been most helpful to its participants.

One woman who had been brought against her wishes to a Bi/Polar seminar by her husband summarized the process of learning to cope in these words: "I have long believed in the saying, 'What a person is born with is God's gift to him; what a person becomes is his gift to God.' I now believe that Bi/Polar is an excellent process of developing a person's personality to the fullest capacity. I'm glad that my husband dragged me into it."

Discussion and Activity Guide

1. Study carefully the suggestions for personal growth for your pattern of strengths, and discuss it with another person.

2. Go through the steps in the plan for growth in the section, "Developing Skills." Work with another person if at all possible. Make a contract with him/her and set a time when you will evaluate together your progress.

3. Go through the steps in the plan again, and continue the process until it has become a part of your life style.

An appropriate plan for reading Chapter 8 is:

1. Read the general material down to the section sub-titled "Patterns One and Three."

2. Go directly to the section which includes your pattern of strengths. Read and study it carefully.

3. Read the sections pertaining to other patterns as an aid in understanding other people.

4. Read the section "Different Ways of Loving."

5. Read the concluding section "Two Laws of Growth."

—8—

Improving Relationships

The real pay-off in learning to cope with life more constructively is improved relationships. It is no accident that participants in Bi/Polar seminars most often express appreciation for the help which they received in dealing with other people. One person's summary is typical: "Knowing who I am and who I think others may be means fewer cross communications, less superficial encounter, and a sense of sharing more quickly reached and more deeply experienced."

My own experience involves six areas of insight and action. *First*, I have realized that some people, especially Pattern Twos and Fours, have real difficulty in relating and I must usually take the initiative in improving my relationship with them. *Second*, I have learned that with aggressive people I need, for their sake as well as my own, to use my independent strength to become more creatively assertive so that I do not accept their domination and then later explode when my resentments build up. *Third*, I know more clearly that there are many people like me—wanting to relate but not always having enough courage to do so—and I know that I must go out of my way to relate to them even when I had rather not. *Fourth*, I have experienced more acceptance when I *do* make the first move instead of waiting for others to do so as my natural inclination directs. *Fifth,* I now understand more fully the importance of expressing appreciation for what other people do—that to provide "strokes" for people is not only important for them but also for me as the initiator. And *sixth,* I am more understanding and accepting of people whose relational needs are not the same as mine.

Most of these learnings for me as a Pattern Three involve *taking more initiative*—using my Independent Risking strength to grow in my greater strength of Dependent Risking. As we will see later, the need of other patterns is quite different.

After the Bi/Polar insights had begun to affect my behavior, I went, as I regularly do, to a conference of Christian educators, held in a retreat setting. My roommate, a Pattern Six, was seldom in the room. In terms of my need—but not his— he was overrelating. My temptation as it always has been was to spend too much time in my room by myself. This time, however, I decided to change my behavior by being more assertive.

When the day's work was over, usually around 9 o'clock in the evening, there were several opportunities for entertainment. One was a soft-drink "night club" where two of my students were helping to provide the entertainment. I wanted very much to go, but it was not the kind of situation where one usually goes alone, and so for the first two nights I went to a film preview room where I could comfortably maintain my anonymity. Then I decided that it was time for me to execute my plan.

I waited in the lobby outside the room where the night club was located to see what would happen. When I saw a group of people I knew, I boldly (for me) asked if I could join them. They seemed glad to have me, and I had a good evening of both entertainment and fellowship with the group. On my second try I simply went in the room, found a table with a vacant place, asked if I could join the group, and again had a great evening.

One Bi/Polar instructor recounts a similar incident with a less happy ending. In a session with clergy, a Pattern One finally exploded in front of some of his colleagues and asked, "Why do the rest of you always do things after our work is done and leave me out?" Those at whom he was pointing the accusing finger looked at one another questioningly, and finally one of them said, "We weren't aware of the fact that we left you out. Some of us just got together and went to a movie last night, but it really wasn't planned. Why didn't you let us know you wanted to go with us?"

What this group of clergy failed to realize was that some people need to be deliberately *included* by others or they will think they are being intentionally *excluded*. The cause of such broken relationships is thoughtlessness. In fewer cases malicious intent is involved. Circumstances that cause disagreement and even enmity are also the cause of much pain. Our direct concern is not the healing of circumstantial divisions, however. Often a third person—a mediator or reconciler—is necessary in such cases, as in labor-management disputes. Rather, we will be dealing with what individuals can do to improve their relationships through the use of their Bi/Polar strengths. The effort may be that of one person only, or it may be (and is much better if it is) a joint effort between the two or more persons involved.

The Importance of Relationships

The need for better relationships exists in all human groupings: the family, the peer group, the work group, the church or synagogue; in small groups and large ones; between neighbors who live in geographic proximity and between nation-states. I am not so unrealistic as to believe that what is said in this chapter will solve all the problems which people have with one another, especially those due to disagreement and conflict. What I have found, however, is that as I begin to understand a person more fully, I am better able to work on whatever conflict we have. So long as I concentrate *only* on the cause of estrangement, I am less likely to find a solution. When I deal with the *person* involved, there is at least the possibility of effective communication.

The importance of this chapter and the one that follows grows out of the relational quality of life. For the religious person the fundamental relation is with God. Even those for whom this is true do not lose their need for human companionship, however. Jesus wisely put in juxtaposition the two commandments: "Love God . . . *and* your neighbor." The two belong together as clearly as sea and seashore. The First Letter of John goes a step further: "If any one says, 'I love God,' and hates his brother, he is a liar; for he who does not love his brother whom he has seen, cannot love God whom he has not seen" (1 John 4:20).

While relationships bring meaning and joy, they also produce pain. Only those who have loved deeply can know the deep pain of losing the loved one by death or other forms of separation. Loving is the basis for both joy and pain, gain and loss, rejoicing and weeping. This chapter goes to the very depths of our being, therefore, by offering help in the increase of satisfaction that arises from involvement with people in a more meaningful way.

While all of us need to belong, some people have a greater need than others. This acknowledgment is one of the distinctive aspects of the Bi/Polar System. We have seen how Patterns Five and Six have the greatest dependency needs, while Patterns Two and Four have the least.

Patterns One and Three also have a high drive for belonging but are often afraid to express it for fear of rejection. Patterns Seven and Eight are more independent than dependent, but even their independence cannot be expressed apart from other people.

So common is this need for others that we recognize the nonrelating person as being abnormal. Hermits have often been the victims of a painful loss which they deal with by not exposing themselves to the further risk of pain.

George Eliot's novel *Silas Marner* is a typical story of this fear. Disillusioned by an unjust conviction for robbery, Silas Marner withdraws into himself and finds his solace in money. Only when his gold is stolen and an abandoned child is left on his doorstep is he freed to resume normal relationships. The story concerns the transformation of Silas Marner as a result of this reinitiation into the world of other people.

Although this is an extreme case, it may be less unusual than it at first appears, especially in our time. Social analysts have often spoken of our age as one of estrangement, or separation. The foundations of society—family, neighborhood, and other natural groupings—have been shaken by the development of an urban, mobile, and often rootless humanity. There were, of course, broken relationships in past generations; in our time there are often no close ties to be broken. Insofar as this is the case, the improving of relationships is not alone the healing of those that are broken but also the initiation of new ones to bring meaning and significance into the lives of lonely human beings.

This chapter, then, is directed toward the use of Bi/Polar insights in the improving of relationships—those that exist but need improving and those that ought to be begun. Using the patterns described in Chapter 5 and the growth process as delineated in Chapter 7, the focus is on how persons with different patterns of strength and varied resources can engage in this process.

A Plan for Improving Relationships

I will first provide in outline form a series of steps to be taken in improving a relationship. Then I will make specific suggestions concerning the strengths, tendencies, and temptations which persons with the various configurations of strengths have in dealing with others. To make this process less cumbersome, I will combine the eight patterns into four clusters. This is possible because the relationships needs, strengths, tendencies, and temptations are almost identical for Ones and Threes, Twos and Fours, Fives and Sixes, and Sevens and Eights.

1. *The first step is to choose a particular relationship on which you want to work.* The other person need not know that you are engaged in such a process. If both are willing to work on the relationship, the battle is half won, of course.

Mary and Jan [1] have been close friends for many years. Recently they found themselves on opposing sides in a school board election. Both were equally strong in their support of opposing candidates. Mary's candidate was pledged to school reform, Jan's to maintain the *status quo.* On one occasion Mary was a speaker for her candidate, who was ill, and Jan was in the audience. Since then Jan has been noticeably restrained on the few occasions when the two have been together. Mary's candidate won, and she received considerable credit for the victory. Mary is a Pattern Seven; she believes that Jan is a Pattern One.

Mary has decided to make a serious effort to heal the division that has arisen because of their recent conflict.

---

[1] Unlike the other situations and cases in this book, this one is contrived to provide an illustration of all the steps in the process.

2. *Think about what you want to receive from the relationship.* This is your motivation for working on it. You may be in pain and want to end the pain. You may have a vision of possibilities not yet actualized in the relationship. Perhaps you realize that the other person could be helpful to you, or you feel that you could be helpful to the other person.

Mary is in real pain because a longstanding friendship has been disrupted. She also recognizes that in the past Jan has been helpful in keeping her life and her interests organized. She believes that Jan is a capable person whose abilities are often not recognized. With Mary's greater assertiveness, she has often been responsible for Jan's self-expression. Before the rupture in their friendship, she had almost convinced Jan that with her children now in high school, it was time she develop additional outlets for her interests and gifts.

3. *Think about what the other person may want to receive from the relationship.* In many instances you can only make a guess about the other person's needs. Even thinking about the other person in this way—trying to enter into his or her situation—is a first step toward improvement, however. Putting yourself in the other's position is often called "empathy."

Jan had always been dependent on Mary for encouragement and motivation. "I suppose I have enjoyed this dependence," Mary is now able to recognize. "It may turn out for the best that our old relationship has been broken. I think Jan is ready to stand on her own, and I must be sure that I do not reestablish the old dependency relationship she had with me." Mary still be-

lieves, however, that Jan needs the "push" that she can provide.

4. *Think about the strengths and resources that you have to contribute to the relationship.*

Mary's independent strength complements Jan's practical/dependent strength. "I am really afraid," Mary muses, "that if someone doesn't continue to activate Jan's independence, she will stagnate. I think I can do that if I don't push too much and am willing to free Jan to be her own person. It may be that she ought not to take a job outside the home as I've been encouraging her to do. She may be better off to find her fulfillment in volunteer work."

5. *Think about the negative forces in your behavior that hinder the relationship.* These negative forces consist especially of the temptations you face in misusing your strengths.

Mary's greatest temptation in her friendship with Jan has been to think that she knows what is best for Jan without really understanding Jan's point of view. On several occasions she had persuaded Jan to become involved in organizations and movements of Mary's choice. She remembered that she had even boasted to her husband that Jan had really blossomed under her sponsorship. "I realize now," she admitted one night, "how much pride I have taken in my ability to manipulate Jan. Perhaps the best thing that she has done recently was to refuse to go along with me when I tried to convince her that she ought to support my candidate in the school board election."

6. *Think about the strengths and resources the other person has to contribute to the relationship.*

As Mary has been sobered by her estrangement from Jan, she has realized how much she had depended, without admitting it, on Jan's stability and organizing ability. "I really need her now as I face a PTA divided by the recent election," she finally admitted. Mary had been elected president of the city-wide PTA prior to the school board election, and she realizes that her aggressive leadership, unless it is tempered by reconciling influences, may only increase the division. "For the first time I'm willing to admit that I really need *her* help," she concludes.

7. *Think about the negative forces in the other person's behavior that hinder the relationship.*

"Jan has really let me run her life far too much," she concludes as she thinks about their past relationship. "She is tempted to avoid conflict, and I know it is going to be difficult for her to discuss our disagreement. I need to recognize *her* natural caution and *my* impulsiveness and see if we can find a meeting ground between the two tendencies."

8. *Think of a time when you gave in to the temptation to misuse your strengths in the relationship.* For Ones and Threes the temptation is often to think too long, to nurse grievances, and to move toward reconciliation too slowly. For Twos and Fours it is to withdraw from the relationship altogether. For Fives and Sixes it is to move impulsively without a well-thought-out plan. For Sevens and Eights the temptation is to believe that an aggressive approach will solve the problem.

Mary did not have to think much about how she had misused her assertiveness in relating to Jan. The most recent example was her assumption, which proved to be incorrect, that Jan would follow her leadership in the school board election. As she considered the past with considerably more thoughtfulness than was her custom, she began to recognize other instances where she had acted in the same manner.

9. *Think of a time when you resisted the temptation to misuse your strengths.*

"I guess it took the sobering affect of a break in our relationship to make me stop long enough to think," Mary observed to her husband one night. "And you've been a great help to me as you have used your Thinking strength to complement mine. I'm glad that you're stronger in Theoretical Thinking than I am. Maybe you can help me think up a plan I can use in improving my relationship with Jan."

10. *Work out a plan for improving the relationship.* The plan must be specific in regard to what you will avoid doing as well as what you will do. The following statements are general in nature: "I will *not* withdraw from the relationship even if I do not feel comfortable about what is happening." "I *will* use my Independent Risking strength to take the initiative in creating opportunities for us to discover one another's interests." "I will *not* come on so strong that I frighten the other person." "I *will* use my Dependent Risking strength to ask for advice." These statements require a specific plan. "I will ask Jan to have coffee with me." "I need help in thinking through this problem, and I will ask Jim for help this morning."

As Mary and her husband continued to talk, they decided that her first step was to ask Jan to come in for coffee and to keep the conversation fairly casual. Mary did this; it was reasonably successful; and they then considered the next step. "I need a good person to be chairperson of the committee for teacher support," Mary said. "The new school board is committed to better classroom teaching, and some of the teachers will have problems in adjusting to the new ways. Jan would be just the person to chair the lay committee that the administration wants for help in making the transition with the established teachers."

This time Mary asked Jan if she could come to her house. When Mary first approached her about the committee, Jan was reluctant to accept the assignment. "You need someone who is fully committed to the changes," she said to Mary. "And you know I have reservations about them."

Mary's impulse was to disagree immediately with Jan's reservation, but she checked her temptation to manipulate Jan into the position. After an unaccustomed pause, she continued. "I've talked with the superintendent and he agrees that you are the person to do the job. We need someone who will understand the teachers' position. The last thing we need is someone like me."

When Jan asked for time to think about the matter, Mary's impulse was to press for an immediate decision. She had realized that Jan needed "thinking space," however, and agreed to the delay.

How did Mary use her strengths in this process? Her motivation was the pain she felt because of her broken relationship with a longstanding friend. She might have dismissed the motivation and gone about her business, but instead she used her Independent Risking to dare look for a solution. As she engaged in Practical Thinking in analyzing the problem, she recognized her need for help in solving it and thus drew upon her husband's greater Theoretical Thinking by using her Dependent Risking to ask his advice. Together they worked out a plan for her to follow, and again she drew upon her Independent Risking to launch the plan and risk herself with another person (Dependent Risking).

For some people this kind of planning may be commonplace, but not for a person with Pattern Seven strengths. It would have been easy for Mary either to have forgotten the conflict, or to have approached Jan directly without taking her feelings into account. As it was she used her own Thinking strengths as well as those of her husband to slow down the natural pace of her movement and approach the situation with an overall plan and strategy.

Naturally not many relationships require the conscious use of this ten-step plan. After it has been followed a few times, in fact, it will become sufficiently familiar that its use will be more or less automatic. Its value is in making us aware that our natural tendencies must sometimes be modified to meet the needs of a particular situation.

Since the manner in which other patterns of strengths use the process is different from that of a Pattern Seven, we will now consider it for each of the four clusters I have previously noted.

Patterns One and Three [2]

Those with Pattern One and Three strengths have a fairly high degree of need for relationships but are often

[2] Additional help in the growth process for the eight patterns will be found in Chapter 7.

reluctant to take the initiative for fear of rejection. Because of their natural cooperative and accepting attitude toward others, they are less likely to have broken relationships than to have unfulfilled ones. They may believe, however, that others take advantage of them (and this may actually be the case), and allow resentments to build up until there is an explosion. They will usually be contrite afterward, and this may be the motivation for their seeking a better way of relating.

The greatest need of Patterns One and Three, moreover, is the ability to accept themselves as persons of worth in relation to others. This is a repeated theme among my respondents. As one woman put it, "Instead of wishing that I was something I was not, I began to realize that *my* strengths were as important as any other's to a relationship, and that I should express them." Another spoke of being "more comfortable in myself and my relationships." ME, whose situation is described in more detail on pages 48, 76, 142 and 143, has found that the affirmation of her strong Theoretical Thinking strength in a nondefensive manner has made it possible for her to take more risks in relationships. By being herself she has received more acceptance from others.

Perhaps the most pressing problem for these two patterns is the developing of consistency in their assertiveness. This is especially true in their dealing with Sevens and Eights. They are often overwhelmed by aggressive people and tend either to back away or, if their frustration level is high enough, to explode. A number of Ones and Threes have reported that before they had learned to express their independence more consistently, this was their only way of getting Sevens and Eights to listen.

Ones and Threes also find it difficult to understand and appreciate the controlled and isolationist stance of Twos and Fours, and often must work to maintain a relationship with them. They generally appreciate the willingness of Fives and Sixes to take the lead in relating but may find it necessary at some point to withdraw to think and plan.

A common temptation for Ones and Threes is to allow others to control their lives and then resent it, often suffering in silence. They often think negatively about themselves and fear rejection because of a belief that they are "unworthy." Their overly cautious attitude may cause them to miss opportunities for helpful relationships, a fact which they later regret.

The contribution of Ones and Threes to relationships grows out of their Thinking strengths. Ones especially bring stability and planning expertise. Threes contribute ideas and help others see possibilities. Both can help slow the impetuosity of those stronger in either Dependent or Independent Risking.

Their lack of assertiveness means that their growth need is to learn to use their Dependent and Independent Risking more fully and creatively. They are often overly serious and can profit from the spontaneity and flair of Fives and Sixes, and may even be stimulated in the exercise of more of these qualities themselves. Twos and Fours can encourage them to be more independent, to be less anxious about pleasing everyone. Twos can be especially helpful in the development of more discipline by Threes, and Fours can provide Ones with new ideas. Sevens and Eights need to encourage them to move more quickly into action.

Improving a relationship is likely to follow one of three patterns in the use of their strengths.

1. Analysis of the problem (Practical Thinking)
   Projection of a possible solution (Theoretical Thinking)
   Receiving support from another person (Dependent Risking)
   Trying out the plan (Independent Risking)
2. Recognition of the problem (Practical Thinking)
   Turning to another for help (Dependent Risking)

Planning a solution (Bi/Polar Thinking)

Moving into action (Independent Risking)

Establishing a better relationship (Dependent Risking)

3. Frustration that leads to asking someone for help (Dependent Risking)

Analyzing the problem and seeking a solution (Bi/Polar Thinking)

Moving into action with the encouragement of the helper (Bi/Polar Risking)

The clue to the growth in relationships of Pattern Ones and Threes is *planning with care*. This step may involve the aid of another person or it may be done alone. They then proceed with caution but also with intentionality, evaluating as they move forward. This is their *natural* style, and when it is self-consciously directed and enhanced with the help of one or more persons, it becomes an effective means of dealing with problems in relationships.

PATTERNS TWO AND FOUR

The natural tendency of Twos and Fours is to want fewer relationships than other patterns, and especially only a few intimate ones. This is the result of their combination of Bi/Polar Thinking and Independent Risking, with their least strength being Dependent Risking.

Their *temptation* is to allow this natural tendency to cause them to withdraw from others, especially when they have developed their Thinking strength and have become polarized on Independent Risking. Ones and Threes are tempted to withdraw because of their fear of rejection— Twos and Fours because of their self-sufficiency which can lead even to a disdain of others less competent than themselves.

I have already cited Dr. Thomas's acknowledged temptation (in Chapter 5) to reject others without pain and, in fact, with considerable self-confidence and self-satisfaction. ST's way of withdrawing (Chapter 7) was to ignore the opinions and decisions of others, even when they should have affected his action. He also found it difficult to accept the constructive criticisms of his colleagues. RC, on the other hand, had tended not to express himself with his business associates because he thought they would not listen to him. The temptation of Twos and Fours is often to go their own way and not interfere with others as the conditions for others not interfering with them.

Twos and Fours have special difficulties in relating to persons with strong dependency needs, especially Fives and Sixes. Twos have problems in accepting the dynamic and imaginative behavior of Eights because they want to keep tighter control over situations than Eights do. On the other hand, Fours are likely to resent the assertive practicality of Sevens and often see Sevens as deliberately trying to repress their imaginative thinking. I have observed Dr. Thomas (Four) and Richard Murray (Seven) many times—a relationship described in Chapter 2—as Murray has reacted negatively to Thomas's suggestions for changes in the details of the Bi/Polar System. Because they have learned to appreciate one another's strengths, however, they persist in their relationships until Murray is convinced of the wisdom of Thomas's ideas or Thomas's ideas are modified by Murray's assertive practicality.

The gift of Twos and Fours to others is their persistence in holding to what they believe to be right. Twos contribute continuity and stability to those stronger in Dependent and Independent Risking. Ones and Threes need the greater order and discipline which Twos bring to life. It is especially difficult for Sixes and Eights to accept this gift regardless of how much they need it, however, because of their natural tendency toward spontaneity and imaginative action. If Twos want to be heard, they must learn to be more tactful and less demanding in relation to others.

The great gift of Fours is in the realm of new ideas. Even Twos may have problems when these ideas upset their established ways of doing things. As Fours deal with Ones, Fives, and Sevens, they must appreciate the natural resistance of these patterns to such ideas and be willing to let the ideas "simmer" instead of pushing for their immediate acceptance.

One need of Twos and Fours in relationships is first of all to recognize their own tendency toward persistence and the likelihood that the tendency will lead to the temptation of obstinacy. That is, strength of conviction can become stubbornness without cavil. A further temptation when their persistence is met with resistance is to withdraw from the relationship. When they do so, their chance of influencing others is markedly decreased.

The first step in improving relationships is therefore a recognition of these realities, especially that an effective expression of one's convictions depends on risking relationships with other people. When they have acknowledged this truth, they are able to use their persistence in a more tactful manner.

Thomas's recognition of his need for the practicality and the action orientation of others has, by his admission, furthered the exposure of his ideas to more people. ST has grown in his openness in expressing his convictions and therefore in influence among his colleagues. RC (see pages 73, 74, and 139) was recently asked to work with me on a project in which I must of necessity provide the leadership. Thinking that he might really not want to bother with it, I asked if he wanted to help in its development. "Yes, I do," was his brief comment, and an indication of growth on his part.

The most common reaction pattern of Twos and Fours is as follows:

    1. Thinking individually about a relationship (Bi/Polar Thinking)

Moving into action (Independent Risking)

Relating more meaningfully to others (Dependent Risking)

For added growth, they need to take an additional step, one which is contrary to their natural inclination, that is, dependence on others.

2. Individual Thinking (Bi/Polar Thinking)

Seeking the help of a trusted friend (Dependent Risking)

Moving into action in relation to others (Bi/Polar Risking)

It is the second step in this formula which must be deliberately chosen. As the growth process continues, this step may be enlarged to include a wider circle. In the process, their Dependent Risking not only grows but their Bi/Polar Thinking and Independent Risking also increase in depth.

Dr. Thomas has described his own pilgrimage, as well as his continued struggle, in words that are representative of Pattern Four:

> I have been aware of my temptation to become polarized on my own ideas and as a result now feel comfortable in drawing on others for Practical Thinking. I have also learned to regard dependence as a value rather than a weakness. Out of this change in my value system, I have learned (now *feel*) more respect for those who have a good supply of dependent strength. I still have the tendency to depreciate dependence but am more willing to express this strength in my own behavior and certainly to appreciate its value more in others.

PATTERNS FIVE AND SIX

Relationships provide the life-blood for Patterns Five and Six. They enter such alliances enthusiastically, maintain them with great enjoyment, and provide acceptance and warmth for others. Unlike Ones and Threes, who want relationships but fear rejection in them, Fives and Sixes just naturally gravitate to people. In Bi/Polar seminars, when participants are divided by patterns, the Fives and Sixes, though they may not have previously known one another, soon form a group that enjoys its work together to a far greater degree than any of the other patterns.

They sometimes forget, in fact, that not everyone cares to spend as much of their time with other people as they do. I remember many years ago when I had a roommate in seminary who was undoubtedly a Pattern Five. Our room was a place where people often dropped by, usually to visit him, not me. Near the end of our two years as roommates, we had a frank talk about one another, at his initiation, of course. His principal criticism of me was that I often had turned to my work while people were still in the room visiting and therefore indicated I really was not interested in people. As a Pattern Three, my academic pursuits took priority over relationships and there came a time when I would follow my natural inclinations. I am not sure I was right or wrong—it does seem a bit impolite, and perhaps I ought to have excused myself and gone to the library. But I do know that I was acting according to what I considered most important at the moment, and so was my roommate. We were just different.

The tendency of Fives and Sixes, of course, is to enjoy people more than anything else; their temptation is to spend so much time with people that they cannot get on with other work. They are especially vulnerable to the accusation that they allow others to rule their lives and determine how they spend their time and energy.

Their problems in relationships often grow out of their failure to appreciate varying degrees of relational needs. Twos and Fours are an enigma to them, for they have difficulty in understanding, much less appreciating, their lack of contacts with people. They may think that Ones and Threes are overly serious, and although they, like Ones and Threes, often have times of low self-esteem, they do not give in to the temptation of *dwelling* on their negative self-image. Usually they will be able to find some diversion to provide what is called in a drama "comic relief," or a change of pace from "heavy drama." They may go to a movie or enjoy their favorite sport when they really should be working on their immediate and long-range problems.

Among the great gifts of Fives and Sixes to other patterns is their ability to provide interest, enjoyment, and flair. Sixes especially have the latter ability, and often have an uncanny sense of when a situation requires comedy. As a Three, I have a special appreciation for what several Fives and Sixes have meant in my life. Had there not been a generous sprinkling of them appearing at various times in my pilgrimage, I think I might long ago have given up the struggle!

The greatest need of Fives and Sixes is to maintain their own identity in relationships. They can easily either become overdependent on others or allow other people to rule their lives. They may become polarized on Dependent Risking and therefore need to be freed to be themselves through the use of Independent Risking in relation to their greatest strength of dependence.

A certain Pattern Five, who has become one of the most effective of our Bi/Polar seminar leaders, had been so polarized on Dependent Risking that he was uncomfortable working with people less relationally inclined. After he became aware of his problem through his participation in Bi/Polar, his other strengths were unblocked so that he was freed to complete an advanced theological degree, a feat that required him to use his least strength, Theoretical Thinking, to an unaccustomed extent.

Another person, a Pattern Six, came to realize that her temptation was to be both dependent on her family and to keep them dependent on her. This knowledge led to a greater use of her other strengths and she has thereby been freed to use her Independent Risking, as she puts it, to "change her life style." Another Pattern Six put it this way:

"I have tended to let my life be run by others—taking on more responsibility that I can manage. Now, in a covenant with my more Practical Thinking wife, I consult with her before taking on an obligation. This helps me eliminate frustration for both of us and for others with whom I am working."

The improving of relationships for Fives and Sixes often begins in this way—with the help of another person who recognizes the danger that even *this* relationship, if not carefully managed, may become an overdependent one. In most of my respondents this has been the case; they need someone to help them think through their problems that are the result of polarization on Dependent Risking. Often the person provides theoretical help for the Five and practical help for the Six in their activating of the Independent Risking strength of the Five or Six.

The process is as follows:

1. Seeking help from another person to get their lives in shape (Dependent Risking)
   Using their Thinking strengths to work out a plan (Bi/Polar Thinking)
   Beginning to take initiative in the better management of their lives (Independent Risking)
   Using both Risking strengths for more realistic relationships (Bi/Polar Risking)

Pattern Fives can begin their own growth by using their Practical Thinking strength.

2. Thinking of a plan for being more realistically relational (Practical Thinking)
   Receiving help from another person for additional ideas (Dependent Risking, Theoretical Thinking)
   Exercising more initiative (Independent Risking)
   Becoming more creatively relational (Bi/Polar Risking)

Pattern Sixes alone will usually begin with Theoretical Thinking and follow this order:

3. Embracing a vision of getting their life in order (Theoretical Thinking)

    Consulting with another to test out their thinking and developing a plan (Dependent Risking, Bi/Polar Thinking)

    Beginning to use more initiative in breaking their dependency role (Independent Risking, Bi/Polar Thinking)

Whatever the process, the end result is to move from polarization on Dependent Risking to the greater use of Independent Risking and both Thinking strengths.

PATTERNS SEVEN AND EIGHT

We have already seen the process at work in Mary, the hypothetical Pattern Seven, earlier in this chapter. The motivating force in her case was pain over losing a long-time friend. Since the natural tendency of Sevens and Eights is to be self-sufficient, there is often a need for unblocking this polarization on Independent Risking before they can recognize their need for more creative relationships, and the pain that Mary felt is one such activating force.

The tendency of Sevens and Eights is to move forward with confidence in their life and work. Their temptation is to believe that they do not need others even though others need them. Patterns One and Three may encourage Sevens and Eights to continue in this illusion by providing a retinue of faithful followers. The dynamic actionist (Seven) and the persuasive visionary (Eight) will almost always draw others to them to become "Yes" people. It may be only when these faithful followers finally get their fill of their leader that the tables are turned.

An extreme example is Adolf Hitler, the leader of Nazi Germany. His apparent neurotic sense of messiahship was not deterred even when some of his close associates began to turn against him and when his insistence on making decisions against the judgment of his generals turned out to be disastrous. The decay in his unmodified sense of power led eventually to what may have been inevitable, his suicide.

I do not mean to imply that Hitler is typical, only that he represents the problems of Sevens and Eights "writ large." More ordinary Sevens and Eights face their own nemesis, however, if they grow in their distrust of others and fail to delegate authority. They gradually become less effective or grow older and discover they can no longer bear the burdens of the world on their shoulders. The dynamic company president is "elevated" to become chairperson of the board, and the more ordinary citizen either lives out his/her life with a sense of relief that he/she no longer must bear the burdens of others, or in frustration that there are no more worlds for him/her to conquer. Some die young from heart attacks, and others respond to a near-fatal attack by slowing down and finding satisfaction in their hobbies or volunteer work.

I do not want to say to Sevens and Eights that they ought to curtail their dynamic leadership. My longstanding envy of their qualities and my recognition of their unique contributions to the political, business, educational, and organized religious life of our society tempers my concern for their *personal* welfare. It is only because their leadership need not be lessened by the development of their other strengths that I am able to continue this section.

For in truth the exercise of their Independent Risking strength need not be lessened—indeed, it can be increased —as they learn to use their other strengths more constructively. For example, when RG (see page 156) learned to his dismay that he had projected a false image of himself among his clergy colleagues he was freed to use his independence more fully. As he recognized that he could not be all things to all people, he was able to be himself more fully and at the same time depend on others. He began to select staff members who complemented his strengths, and he also recognized that he could use his independence for more self-discipline and set up a regular study time which improved his preaching. Other people I have known have grown in their other strengths by a selective process involving a trust relationship with one or a few people whom they respect and on whom they come to depend.

Dynamic persons sometimes begin to depend on others only after their influence lessens. What I am proposing is that they recognize their need before this occurs. As one Seven put it, Bi/Polar has helped him understand what idolatry means. His idols were his self-sufficiency and his belief that no one else could quite measure up to his own ability to function. In another case a Pattern Eight seminary student who thought of himself as highly relational (and he was a Warm Eight) heard what others said about him through the Bi/Polar inventories and began to depend on others to supplement his strengths. Two of my most enjoyable Bi/Polar seminars have been with his coleadership.

Another Pattern Eight male had really feared his independence in his church profession, partly because his youth had made others suspicious of his tendencies. A Bi/Polar seminar helped him affirm his Independent Risking and Theoretical Thinking strengths and at the same time made him aware of his need for drawing upon others for practicality. In the case of a Pattern Eight woman, motivation came from being confronted with the reality of her temptation to be impatient, her compulsion to talk, and her extreme confidence in the rightness of her position. She also came to see that she threatened others, especially because of her sex, and that she had to *risk* in order to have better relationships. "Just having this awareness," she writes, "plus having been given methods to control these qualities, has made for big steps forward."

Once the realization is activated, one of the following processes is viable.

1. Pattern Seven

   The willingness to risk a new life style (Independent Risking)

   Analysis of the problem and dependence on others for ideas (Dependent Risking, Practical Thinking, Theoretical Thinking)

   Initiation of new patterns of behavior (all strengths)

   Growth in Dependent Risking

2. Pattern Eight

   Willingness to risk (Independent Risking)

   A vision of what might be (Theoretical Thinking)

   Dependence on someone in helping work out a plan (Dependent Risking, Practical Thinking)

   Moving ahead (Independent Risking)

3. Pattern Seven

   Thinking through the situation; analyzing the problem (Practical Thinking)

   Consulting others for ideas (Dependent Risking, Theoretical Thinking)

   Moving ahead with a plan (Practical Thinking, Independent Risking)

4. Pattern Eight

   A vision of a more satisfactory life (Theoretical Thinking)

   Working out a plan with another person (Practical Thinking, Dependent Risking)

   Moving ahead (Independent Risking)

There is, of course, no one order of using one's strengths. The crucial matter is that all of them are used.

Different Ways of Loving

We have now concluded the major emphasis of this chapter: the presenting of a general plan for improving relationships and the making of suggestions for the four clusters of patterns of strengths. There is still another purpose, however, and it involves a deeper understanding of the ways in which people with different strengths relate to others.

First I want to pose this as a question based on the biblical injunction to love one's neighbor: Is everyone called to love the neighbor in the same manner? There has been a strong tendency in the Jewish-Christian tradition to answer the question affirmatively, and the emphasis has been on the expression of love that grows out of Dependent Risking alone. I do not refer to human dependence on God, for that way of understanding the human situation reflects a recognition of the radical difference between Creator and creature. The Bi/Polar System maintains this view of the Creator/creature relationship as much for the person whose greatest strength is Independent Risking as for those who are strongest in the other strengths.

What I mean is that Christian love has often been sentimentalized, or in Bi/Polar terms it has been polarized on Dependent Risking without reference to the other strengths. This, I believe, is due to a misunderstanding of the meaning of love. *Agape*, the Greek word usually used in the New Testament and translated as "love," is unlike another Greek word, *philia*, which also means "love." *Philia* refers to a spontaneous, natural affection, emotional in quality and not involving thinking. *Agape*, on the other hand, is based on esteem, or holding another in high regard; it is *active good will*, involving truth and an act of the will, not necessarily including personal affection. To love one's neighbor, or in Bi/Polar terms to enter into constructive relationships, includes—as does the first commandment (love of God)—mind, heart, soul, and strength.

That is, loving the neighbor means using all one's strengths. Although it involves Dependent Risking, it does not mean becoming dependent on the other person or making him/her dependent. The purpose of this kind of love is to free both persons to be more fully themselves. Loving God, in fact, is not what makes us dependent on him; rather, such love frees us to be ourselves and to express our respect to God in active good will to others.

There is no better illustration of this meaning of Christian love than the one Jesus uses in Luke 10. A lawyer comes to Jesus and asks how he may have eternal life. Jesus asks the lawyer what the Law (Torah) says, and the lawyer quotes the two great commandments, "Love God . . . and love your neighbor. . . ." Jesus approves of the answer, and the lawyer then asks, "And who is my neighbor?"

Jesus then tells the story to which we have affixed the title, "The Good Samaritan." The neighbor, the Samaritan, is first moved with pity (or compassion) when he sees the man who has been robbed. There is no record that he made any effort to enter into a friendly relation with the victim; he does what needs to be done at the moment. He gives the victim first aid and takes him to an inn, makes sure his needs will be cared for, and then leaves! One can speculate that the Samaritan was a Pattern Two or Four, not a Five or Six. He did what he could to meet the immediate need of the neighbor, and then went about his business, promising to pay any additional expense when he would return to the inn later.

I recognize that I am drawing from this parable conclusions which are not its major point, that point being that anyone we meet is our neighbor. I think it is not reading into the story a meaning which is not there, however, when I conclude that God expects us to use what we have been given in relation to others and that this is not the same for all persons.

There is an additional conclusion we can draw from the commandment itself. "You shall love your neighbor as yourself" means that self-esteem and esteem of neighbor go together. Contemporary psychologists are right, I believe, in insisting that we cannot love others unless we have both been loved and love ourselves, that is, have esteem and respect for ourselves.

The word that has come to me through the Bi/Polar System—a word that has been made explicit in this chapter—is a clearer understanding that *the way we love others is not the same for all people*. We bring different gifts and graces to life, both in whom we were born to be and whom we have become. In this chapter we have concentrated on the expression of our *natural* tendencies and how they can both deteriorate and fructify.

For most of my life I have chafed under the knowledge that I could not relate to other people and approach life in the same way that other people do. I wondered why this was the case and sometimes resented my lot. Why, for example, could I not provide the sparkle and natural warmth that one of my sisters gave to others? I sensed—but had no way of explaining why—that she was who she was not because she had earned it but because it had come to her as a gift, a gift that I did not have.

And I resented for quite a long time my wife's dynamic qualities that often made her a star in relation to others. Not only could she do things that I tried but failed to do, she also received recognition more readily than I did. It was easier for her to make friends, for example, though friends were not as important to her as for me. What I have come to realize is that who she is also came as a gift and was not something she earned. I do not mean that she has not developed her gift, but I have seen more clearly that both of us, in our own and quite different ways, have our separate callings in life, and that she needs me just as much as I need her.

Late in life we became the foster parents of a teenager whose individuality was described under Pattern Six in Chapter 5. In my relation to him—for less than nine years before he died of cancer—I came to realize that while he brought joy and flair to my life, he needed my stability and serious nature fully as much as I needed his love of life and marvelous sense of humor. Had he lived, I think we would have gone on needing one another, hopefully not as a son dependent on a father but as two adults able to be supportive, freeing, and complementary of one another.

Much of this I had sensed before I came to know the Bi/Polar System, but I know it much more clearly now and am able to accept it more happily. I understand more fully that all of us have both needs and gifts, and that they are not, and we need not try to make them, the same. In his great wisdom the Creator has made us to complement one another, not to be duplicates.

To return to the biblical image, we show our esteem for our neighbor in different ways. Some are naturally reconcilers but need to grow in their ability to stand on their own convictions. Others are more self-sufficient, provide the conviction which others do not have, and need to find more creative ways of relating. Still others are more self-sufficient, are actionists, show their love of neighbor in more active ways, and need to grow in esteem for others. Some people provide stability in relationships, make their contribution through a steady and dependable kind of living, and need help in learning to act more decisively.

I do not mean to imply that we cannot grow in the way we relate to people. The central purpose of this chapter has been to indicate how the various patterns of strength can do this. But we move from where we are and we do not become identical with someone who acts out of a different set of gifts.

Some of us will still fulfill our purpose in life primarily through ideas, others through dealing with practical problems, others through warm and enduring relationships, others through doing. If we could only recognize and accept this fact, we could live in greater harmony with one another. For example, many of the disagreements that arise between religious people result from the failure to recognize that we have a variety of gifts. Paul put it better than I can in his statement: "There are varieties of gifts but the same Spirit; and there are varieties of service, but the same Lord; and there are varieties of working, but it is the same God who inspires them all in every one" (1 Corinthians 12:4–6).

Two Laws of Growth

The emphasis in this chapter has been on beginning with who we are and on allowing others to be who they are. We must also become who we were intended to be, and that involves the investing of our natural inclinations in the process of total living. The first step is self-esteem; the second is esteem of others. Becoming polarized on our natural inclination can lead only to decay and deterioration. The first law of growth is to accept and affirm ourselves, the second is to invest who we are in the process of creative living in order to become our best selves. The second law involves the painful process of unblocking the use of our lesser strengths and freeing ourselves from the idols that our greater strengths build.

But the beginning point of growth is to accept ourselves as we now are, and *then* move out to use our gifts more creatively and constructively.

Some years ago a beloved friend and my personal physician wrote to my dean to assure him that I had been influential in his life and the lives of others even though he knew I would never receive the recognition that some of my colleagues do. At the time I was unable to appreciate fully what this friend had done. I can accept it now—with gratitude and with a sense of the truth of what he wrote. And one of the major reasons I can do so is that the Bi/ Polar System, on which this book is based, has made me aware of the different ways we express our love of God and neighbor.

At the beginning of this book I said that it is a religious book even though it does not often use religious terminology. And I believe this is true. Its plan is a tool to help us express our religious faith in our own language, using our particular gifts in our own way, and increasing in all our strengths as we express our true individuality in a constructive and expanding manner. In this way we are responding to God's gifts to us and finding ways of adding works to our faith.

Many parts of the book, I am sure, seem tiresome, even tedious and pedantic. I know no other way to say some of the things that I must say to make the concepts and the plan clear. But I hope this basic religious quality—life-giving and life-enriching—shows through, and that from it your own faith in yourself, in others, and in God, and your relation to yourself, to others, and to God will increase.

Discussion and Activity Guide

1. Study the material on improving relationships for your own pattern of strengths, and discuss it with another person.

2. Go through the steps of the "Plan for Improving Relationships," discussing them with another person if possible. Work on a specific relationship. Contract with your partner to meet several weeks later to evaluate your progress.

3. Continue using the plan until it has become a part of your way of relating to people.

4. On the basis of the section, "Different Ways of Loving," decide how you can best implement the injunction to love your neighbor as yourself. Discuss this with another person.

5. How can you best follow the "Two Laws of Growth"?

–9–

Using Your Insights
in Groups

During my professional career, I have had several colleagues with whom I found it difficult to work. "If only they would accept another position!" I have found myself thinking, and perhaps even daring to say it aloud. "Life would be so much more pleasant if I just had pleasant people to work with."

Well, some of them have gone elsewhere, and some have retired; but I have found that this did not solve my problems in group relationships. At times it seemed that the persons who replaced them were even more difficult, and so I still had to learn to work with people who, I sometimes wished, would just go away and leave me in peace.

It is not alone in working relationships that people have such problems. Marriage and the family, which can be and often is the most rewarding of all human communities, can also become a cauldron of hate and spite. The accelerating divorce rate during recent decades indicates that husbands and wives often find it easier to break a relationship than to learn how to live together. Many are searching for the ideal marriage partner, and the incidence of second divorces indicates that their second attempt is often no more successful than the first. Similarly, strained parent-child relationships have many causes, but an important one is the unrealistic expectations that parents often have of their children.

It is *not* always easy to function as a member of a team —at work, in marriage and the family, in peer groups— and we seldom find the ideal group. Sometimes the struggle to build a good group is more than we are willing to venture. Most people do want to have better relationships, however, and one thing is sure: this will not happen by accident. It is only when we use our gifts and strengths for the building of human community that creative groups emerge.

We might remember the words of Shakespeare in *Julius Caesar.* "The fault, dear Brutus, is not in our stars but in ourselves. . . ." This is not to suggest that all the fault is ours if a business falters, a marriage falls apart, or a family becomes a place of friction rather than love. Nevertheless, we do bear a responsibility for improving group relationships, and we may be the only person willing to take on the task of doing something about them.

I will always remember a story told by a psychotherapist to a class many years ago. A woman had come to him to talk about her problems with her husband. The therapist became convinced as she talked that the fault was primarily her husband's. He reminded her of two things, however: that bad relationships are seldom the responsibility of one person alone, and that regardless of who was wrong in this situation, she was the one who seemed willing to work on it.

Some time later the therapist saw the woman again. "You've saved my marriage," she said to him in gratitude. "I began to work on the ways in which you helped me see I was to blame, and as I did so my husband began to change, ever so slightly. He isn't a completely different person, but there has been enough response in him and enough change in me that our marriage has improved greatly."

There is no guarantee, of course, that all such occasions will work out as happily as this one did, but the story does have universal application. As we work on our part of the blame, perhaps the other person will respond positively to what we are doing.

We will be thinking about group relationships in this chapter and seeing how Bi/Polar insights apply to such groups. The examples pertain to two kinds of groups: first, staff relationships—in business, church, or other situations —and second, marriage and the family. The principles can be adapted for all kinds of groups, however.

STAFF RELATIONSHIPS

Any organization that has two or more people working for it has a staff. Sometimes these people must work quite closely together. This is true of a business, a team of workers, a church, the administration of a school, college, or university, and any other group where the doing of its work depends on cooperative endeavor. Members of a faculty, unless they are doing team-teaching, can do their work with considerable autonomy because much of it is done in a classroom. So it is with a group of lawyers, doctors, or other professionals. Some communication is required, of course, but much of their work can be done individually.

Even when such autonomy is easily maintained, however, the work of the *group* is often hurt because of the lack of good working relationships. For example, when teachers go their own way (as I have seen them do), the work of the school is hindered regardless of how well they do their own thing. Students begin to sense the presence of friction, and they may begin to take sides. I know of one faculty some years ago where the relationship with the dean was so bad that another person had to be called in to preside over faculty meetings so that the common work of the school could be planned. It was not an especially desirable place to be!

Church and Business Staffs

The two kinds of staffs in which Bi/Polar has been most fully utilized are business and the church. We noted in Chapter 2 that the System was born as Dr. Thomas worked as a psychological consultant for business. He discovered early in his work that business enterprises need some people who are higher in Thinking and others in Risking in order to prosper. These two strengths were first designated broadly as stability (Thinking) and dynamism (Risking).

As Dr. Thomas refined his system, he identified, as we have previously seen, the eight basic patterns of strengths. Not all patterns are necessary even for a large staff; the more that are represented the healthier the enterprise can become. Persons representing each pattern have their own unique contributions to make to a staff. These contributions, in shorthand form, are as follows:

Pattern One: Stability, dependability, and cooperativeness;

Pattern Two: Order, discipline, and persistence;

Pattern Three: Ideas, consideration of others, and synthesizing ability;

Pattern Four: Innovative ideas, persistence, and creativity;

Pattern Five: Warmth, reconciling ability, and practicality;

Pattern Six: Flair, warmth, and responsiveness to others;

Pattern Seven: Initiative, action, and practicality; and

Pattern Eight: Innovative thinking, initiative, and dynamism.

We have seen repeatedly how problems can arise out of the expression of these different patterns of strengths when there is no reference to the needs and strengths of others. When strengths are misused, the problems are much greater.

These problems may often seem to be—and in fact are—petty matters. In one church staff of three, the pastor was a Pattern Four who naturally prized his privacy. In an open session after the three had been through a Bi/Polar seminar, they began to tell one another what was especially irritating in the behavior of one another. "Do you know what really bugs me?" the pastor asked of the other two. "No, I'm sure you don't because you wouldn't do it if you did. Well, I'll tell you," he went on to say; "it's when you go out of my office after a conference and leave the door open."

To most people this may seem trivial to the point of being ridiculous, but it was not so for the pastor with Pattern Four strengths. It was an annoying and unsettling failure on the part of his staff to respect his privacy. When I heard this story, I began to wonder if it is an unconscious recognition of this need that makes so many students, when they leave *my* office after a conference, ask me if I want them to leave the door open or close it. Frankly, I couldn't care less, and it is almost, but not quite, irritating to me that they ask.

In other instances the cause of conflict is much deeper. Not long ago a friend came to talk about his problems in a new position. He had recently been employed as administrative manager of a firm whose president, probably a Pattern Eight, seemed unbearably "sloppy" to my Pattern Two friend in the way he conducted his business. My friend's job description called for him to reorganize the firm, and he was determined, out of his Pattern Two need for order and discipline and his natural persistence, to do so. What I felt compelled to say to him was that he had to slow down, to take one step at a time, and to realize that a business which had previously had no such order—but needed it badly—could not be remade overnight.

Whether this company president, without the benefits of Bi/Polar insights, instinctively knew that he needed the gifts of my friend I have no way of knowing. In other instances business staffs have been remade on the basis of the principle of diversified gifts and strengths.

Planning for Staff Personnel

One company has had for several years a Pattern Two president. When he came to the firm there was not a single dynamic person in top management positions. Gradually the president has deliberately replaced these people, as they have retired or been placed in comparable positions in the firm, with persons having Pattern Seven strengths. He has also employed a Pattern Four technical aid who is full of new ideas; a public relations manager with Pattern Five strengths to relate to outsiders; and others with strengths that particularly fit their positions. As a result, the profits of the firm have increased dramatically.

This same principle of operation has also been used in church staffs.

RG, (see pages 156f. and 187), a Pattern Seven, has used Bi/Polar inventories of strengths and personal interviews as the basis for building his ministerial staff. To complement his own practical dynamism, he selected a Pattern Eight, who, as RG puts it, has more ideas than he can possibly put into practice. He is assertive and dynamic and pushes to get things under way but needs RG's greater practicality for his ideas to be implemented. The other associate chosen is a Pattern Three, who thinks things through carefully, helps RG plan ahead and consider goals and future possibilities, and continually supplies him with reading material pertinent to matters they are considering. As RG, with candid and perceptive insight puts it, "I know quite well what

I need from others and what others need from me."

In church situations where there is no professional staff —only a pastor and perhaps a secretary—the lesser strengths of the pastor can be complemented by lay people carefully chosen. Often a pastor will tend to choose those who are like himself. Rather, he should proceed on the opposite principle and deliberately select lay staff who are different in order to have a maximum representation of all the strengths.

One of my respondents provides an example of how this principle worked. After completing a Bi/Polar seminar, he went home and selected seven dynamic women who completed in one week a job that he had been neglecting for months. The pastor's least strength was Practical Thinking, and he needed—and needs—lay people with this strength in abundance to complement his relational skills and Theoretical Thinking.

One-to-One Relationships

Another kind of contribution that the insights of this book can make to staff relationships consists of improving one-to-one relationships—the emphasis of Chapter 8. One of my Pattern Seven respondents (MH) recounts the problem he had with a staff member, a Pattern Three (CJ), who had been on the staff some time before his appointment as principal pastor. The new pastor discovered during his first six months that CJ did not speak up during staff meetings concerning her disagreements with staff decisions but would then countermand them by ignoring them in what she did.

MH was tempted to avoid conflict—he has a Pattern Five principal blend—by ignoring the matter. His better judgment and practicality made him decide that this was unwise. He confronted CJ with his perception that she seemed to want to subvert his role as principal pastor of the church. She denied this allegation. "I really need the creative perception that you can bring to our situation," MH assured her, "but I need it before a decision is made, not after. I also think," he added, "that you need my Risking strength to help move the church toward a more dynamic ministry."

CJ was at first "hurt" because she interpreted MH's action as critical of her work. But then she began to think about what he had said, and over the next few months she took seriously MH's need of her and her need of his dynamism. The result has been not only a good relationship and forward movement by the church; it has also led to CJ's personal growth. As MH puts it: "Her body-carriage looks healthier and stronger; there is joy in her facial lines. She has lost little time due to illness, and she puts more good 'head stuff' in staff process. The growth of the church reflects these inner dynamics."

General Improvement

When there are no major problems in staff relationships, a deeper understanding by members of both themselves and others can lead to a general overall improvement of staff productivity. This was the case in a large church staff that Dulaney Barrett as a Doctor of Ministry student at Perkins School of Theology studied for his doctoral project.[1] What occurred in this instance is reflected in typical remarks made by staff members. "The Bi/Polar affirmation of my strengths has given me more confidence to express myself in staff meetings." "It helps me not to have false expectations of other staff members." "It helped us affirm and seek for the expression of other peoples' strengths." "It helped me work with a person who is less practical than

---

[1] This project report is on file at Perkins School of Theology, Southern Methodist University, Dallas, Texas.

I am, and I can affirm this person's Theoretical Thinking."
"It helped me accept the fact that some people need to
think things through longer than I do." "Bi/Polar helped
me learn to compromise when needed and not to try to
manipulate others." "It's great to feel more acceptance of
my creativity." "It has encouraged me to risk my ideas
with others."

What all of these comments indicate is that many people have been able to accept and express themselves more
fully and at the same time affirm and accept others. Differences have been both acknowledged and celebrated
more completely.

In other instances the greatest need is for some staff
members to exercise more fully the pattern *blends* that
correspond to their basic pattern of strengths.[2]

Using Pattern Blends

One pastor whom I have known for many years is generally considered by those who work with him to be a Pattern Seven—"assertive and enterprising." In a seminar
in which the staff of which he was then principal pastor
took part, his inventory showed him to be a Pattern Five
—"outgoing and practical." The result was largely due to
his own perception of himself and that of his wife. "Only
my wife and I know who I really am," he observed. "I'm
basically a highly relational person." Thinking back to the
early days of my friendship with him, I could believe this
was the case. As an associate pastor, this had certainly been
the strength he had manifested. In the church situation
in which the seminar was held, however, he was exercising
his Pattern Seven blend, because it was a situation which
called for dynamic assertiveness and there were few such
dynamic people on the staff. My friend was deliberately
using his own assertiveness to a higher degree than was
natural for him to serve the needs of the situation.

---

[2] Pattern blends are considered in Chapter 5.

With the knowledge on which this book is based, a staff can also deliberately bring out of one another the fullest expression of strengths. In another large church staff, the principal pastor was a Pattern Three and was known for his well-thought-out and prepared sermons. The minister of education was the dynamic risker, and this showed in the extensive and dynamic teaching ministry of the church. One of the associate pastors was a Pattern Four —the creative, innovative thinker. The burden of the staff's deliberation in the seminar was an attempt to deal with the particular gifts of this person. "How can we help this creative person use *his* strengths for local church ministry?" they kept asking themselves. They drew up a plan which involved each of them using his creative ability as a consultant—both to enhance their work and to fully utilize his strengths.

Placement

A knowledge of where a person's strengths lie can also be used for placement purposes. In one instance, a group of clergy persons along with their administrative leader participated in a seminar together. One young man, a Pattern Three, had already been asked, contrary to his better judgment, to begin a new congregation in the area. After the seminar, he went to the administrator and said: "See, I told you I wasn't the right person to begin a new church. You need someone more dynamic than I am to do that." The administrator responded positively, appointed this man to an associate position, and chose a different kind of person to begin the new congregation.

All of what has been said concerning a professional staff is also applicable to the lay staff of a voluntary agency such as the church. The one illustration which I used earlier indicates the principle which is crucial: the professional or professionals look for lay people who complement their own strengths. For example, if pastors are not skilled in financial matters, they can depend on lay persons for this work (a Pattern One or Two in most instances). More reserved pastors will become the trainers of evangelists and seek those who are outgoing and dynamic for the actual work of evangelism. If their own strength is slanted toward the dynamic, they may need a lay assistant to help with the work of organizing and enabling the lay staff. Where can such people be found? One largely untapped source of voluntary help consists of retired people who have the time and sometimes the inclination to give large blocks of time to the church and other service agencies.

With regard to the church, this principle of operation is sound not only practically but also theologically. According to the New Testament, the church is the *whole* People of God. The key statement in 1 Peter 2:9 is repeated in many ways in other passages: "But you are a chosen race, a royal priesthood, a holy nation, God's own people, that you may declare the wonderful deeds of him who called you out of darkness into his marvelous light." It is not always that a practical reality and a biblical truth coincide so beautifully as they do in this basic understanding of the nature of the church.

MARRIAGE AND FAMILY RELATIONSHIPS

The other group where Bi/Polar has been most widely used is in marriage and the family. I have found in my own experience and through counseling with others that one of the most acute problems in the family is that spouses expect one another to be someone other than who they are. The same is true of parents and children: parents either expect their children to be like them, or they attempt to fulfill their own aspirations through their children. A father wants his son to be athletic when the son is not so inclined. A mother expects a daughter to fit the social stereotype (which, to be sure, is changing) of the submissive woman, but the daughter is dynamic and enterprising. The broken lives and broken relationships because of false expectations both of spouses and of parents are legion.

One man put it this way:

My wife is a Pattern One; I am a Pattern Five. She thinks about issues and does not want to talk quickly. I want to talk things through immediately, to settle an issue without waiting. Whereas I demand immediate solutions, she needs time for deliberation. As a consequence, she has thought me to be impetuous and demanding, and I have considered her moody and depressed.

As we began to understand our natural inclinations, we realized that we were simply being who we are. I do not mean that we do not still have problems, for we *are* who we are. But there is an added dimension of *awareness* we did not previously have. In the midst of my impatient demands, I remember my own nature as well as hers. The result is that we have moved in the direction of each other. Still exhibiting the same general tendencies, we are not quite so bound to our own way. I can laugh at myself about things that I once considered a matter of principle. This has helped us know how to live with one another with our particular approaches to human relationships, *using* our strengths but mindful of limitations created by the needs of the other.

Husband-Wife Relationships

The following case shows how opposites can supplement one another's strengths in marriage:

In our marriage, I am the idea person, she the practical realist. I was once hurt and angry at the way she "shot down" all my wonderful ideas. Now we have learned how to work together. She supplies reality testing and I supply possibilities. It works!

In another instance a husband wrote:

I am better able to respect my wife's need for privacy (Pattern Four) and she is more understanding of my need for socializing (Pattern Six). While we have gained appreciation of our differences, we are also more appreciative of the things we share, such as love for new ideas. In short, our relationship is deepening as a result of our continuing participation in Bi/Polar.

In summary, marriage partners find the most helpful part of the principles on which this book is based to be an understanding, acceptance, and affirmation of one another's differences. Some also find that it enhances their sharing of what they have in common. As they make these two movements, their own relationship is enhanced and they are able to face their problems with other people more creatively. As one man put it: "I have tended to let my life be run by others, taking on more responsibilities than I can manage. Now in a covenant with my more Practical Thinking wife, I consult her before taking on an obligation." And another put it simply: "Bi/Polar has helped me stop arguing about whose way is *best!*"

Parents and Children

The relationships between parents and children can be just as dramatically changed when parents are willing to accept their children as they are. I do not mean that parents need to or should be overly permissive by failing to provide discipline and standards for children. There is a wide difference between allowing children to express their real individuality and failing to direct that individuality into constructive channels. Indeed, understanding their individuality provides the basis for knowing *how* a child will respond most readily to discipline. Some children need a "heavy hand" (those who are naturally assertive); others need "strokes" (those who are highly relational); still others can more easily "reason together" with their parents.

What we *are* concerned with is the common tendency of parents to try to make their children fit their preconceived patterns of feeling, thinking, and behavior. One of my respondents (see LT, pages 88 and 152) expressed the problem in this way:

The Bi/Polar "Ah ha!" changed my family relationships. That insight concerned my previous attempts to make them conform to my image of what a wife and children should be. I had been trying to make my Pattern Three wife more sociable and resented the fact that she did not like the many friends that I, as a Pattern Six, made. I was also trying to make my Pattern Four son into a copy of myself. He is an idea person and I thought he was not active enough. I am an ex-hurdler, a former cheer leader, a motorcycle rider, and a sports car fan. His interests are art, music, and language. The only person whom I accepted for what she was was my highly relational daughter; she was the only "o.k." person at home.

When I returned home from my first Bi/Polar seminar, I called my wife and children together and apologized for my attempts to remake them. I told them I was "getting off their necks" and would stay off. That was four years ago, and my son still recalls that day as his "day of independence." My wife has blossomed under my willingness to let her work out her own social relationships and has almost literally become a new person.

A similar situation is provided by a Pattern One father and Pattern Five mother in dealing with their Pattern Four son.

I simply could not comprehend our family relationships. While there was nothing "rocky" about them, I just couldn't understand them. My wife, it seemed to me, did some awfully "dumb" things without thinking, and our boy was always coming up with crazy far-out ideas that drove his mother berserk and caused my very practical mind to fly off into all kinds of frustrations.

When John was eleven, he expressed a desire for an electric train. I thought it was a reasonable idea, but his mother thought it unnecessary. John had a pretty good idea of what he wanted; so I bought him a set for Christmas—about a $30.00 set.

My concept of an electric train was some track laid in a circle with a train that would go round and round and perhaps a few houses and other things to give it some special effects. I was soon to learn the difference between an electric toy train and a model railroad.

For about a year a battle raged. John was gearing up to carry out a mind-boggling plan for his model railroad. Ideas were flowing forth like a Texas gusher. Every time he received a model railroad magazine, he either had an extension of a former idea or else he took off on a whole new set. I just couldn't handle it all because what I wanted him to do was get the railroad finished and running.

About six months after this all began, my wife and I went to a Bi/Polar seminar. John came to the conclusion on the basis of what he was learning about the system that he was a Pattern Four.[3]

[3] John and his parents were later in a seminar I conducted, and the result of his inventories confirmed that he was a Pattern Four. At fourteen years of age, he was the first, and sometimes only person to grasp some of the more subtle ideas of the seminar.

When we began to talk about what this meant, a whole new world opened up.

What our family consisted of was a wife/mother who was high in relationships with her least strength in ideas and a husband/father who is above all things practical. Out of that marriage had come an offspring who blew the whole thing open by being theoretical and independent with his Practical and Dependent strengths least.

That *was* something to work on! Knowing where each of us is, however, we *can* work on it. Each of us is aware that the other family members bring something unique to our home. We accept the major strengths of the other members, and the continued frustrations that go with it, and we accept the fact that we each have areas where we are less strong and try not to have expectations beyond that person's capabilities. I believe each of us is showing growth in our areas of lesser strengths as we relate to one another.

In the meantime John's train has filled a large room, and it remains incomplete. Regularly a whole new direction is opened up in model railroading and mother and father grin and bear it.

In staff relationships it is relatively easy to make shifts in responsibilities, changes in personnel, and adjustments in job descriptions. Husbands and wives can solve their problems in a similar way by deciding to end their relationship, but this often creates more problems than it solves. Our society does not much approve of parents' turning in their children for models that meet their expectations more fully. In no place is acceptance and affirmation of one another more essential than in the family.

The cases that have been used are indicative of what happens when false expectations are modified. The leopard cannot change its spots, but the leopard can be trained and its true character can be channeled. To accept other family members as God made them is an important step toward more creative marriage and family relationships.

A PLAN OF ACTION

Thus far we have considered specific situations with conclusions related to them. It is now appropriate to generalize on the basis of these examples concerning how group relationships can be made more creative. Not all of these principles are appropriate for every situation.

1. *Where possible, members of groups should be chosen so that their strengths complement one another.*

This is especially important with regard to a staff. The principle might also be applied to a study group in which a mix of Theoretical and Practical Thinking could help the group consider both theory and application. I am *not* suggesting that marriages should be based on a deliberate selection of a spouse in this manner! A prior knowledge of where strengths lie is a good starting point for a marriage, however, and the Bi/Polar system is being used by marriage counselors in this way.

2. *Persons should as nearly as possible be given responsibilities commensurate with their major strengths.* Although this is not always feasible, it is still an apt principle. This was the case of the Pattern Three clergyman whose assignment was changed from starting a new church to membership on a church staff. Other less obvious examples occur in the cases cited: for example, the Pattern Four associate pastor who was made a consultant to other staff members as the idea person. Even in marriage and the family there is a sense in which the principle works. An example is the man who uses his wife as a consultant to keep him from assuming more obligations than he can carry responsibly.

This principle does not imply that we must fit our work or family assignment precisely. We have seen in previous chapters how lesser strengths can be increased along with major ones. With sufficient self-discipline, we can do a wide variety of tasks and fill many roles, and the exigencies of life often call us to do so. The price we often pay, however, is frustration, dissatisfaction, and reduced productivity.

Nor is there any particular virtue in doing what we do not want to do just for the sake of doing it. There may be good reasons for such self-discipline, of course. I do not especially like the idea of doing a small amount of jogging most mornings, but I usually do so because of the inherent value in such exercise. There are other forms of exercise which I dislike more, and so I choose the one that is most satisfying.

The principle of fitting people with tasks commensurate with their major strengths, therefore, stands—where feasible. I have added "where feasible," however, because I have found that there are some things I must do in spite of my dislike for them so that I can do the things that my natural tendencies cause me to enjoy. That is a part of life, and I know few people who can do only what they like. There is both practical and theological wisdom in a statement from the United Methodist "Covenant Service."

> Christ has many services to be done; some are easy, others are difficult; some bring honor, others bring reproach; some are suitable to our natural inclinations, and temporal interests, others are contrary to both. In some we may please Christ and please ourselves; in others we cannot please Christ except by denying ourselves. Yet the power to do all these things is assuredly given us in Christ, who strengthens us.[4]

The point is that we are enabled to do what is not especially to our liking more zestfully if we are in a situation where, by and large, we like what we are doing.

These first two principles require a certain amount of choice for fulfillment, either in the selection of people for particular jobs or in shifting responsibilities within existing groups. Those that follow are more fully applicable to existing groups. They are stated in the imperative as means you can employ in working toward better expressions of human community.

---

[4] *The Book of Worship for Church and Home of The United Methodist Church* (Nashville, Tennessee: The Methodist Publishing House, 1964), p. 387.

3. *Understand what you actually do in a particular group of people.* This principle does not ask you to decide why, only *what.* That is, how do you behave with regard to the people with whom you work, in your family, or in some other group?

In your family, keep a record (in writing if possible) for a week of what you did in relating to each family member. It will be helpful if you have an ally who helps you be honest and more objective concerning your behavior.

In a staff situation, keep a similar record both of meetings together and of individual relationships. For example, every time you talk in a staff meeting, make a mark on paper. Or you may want to have what group theorists call a "process observer" keep the record on yourself and others. It is not only how many times you talk but also *how* you speak that is important—in anger, impatience, and so on. Also keep a record of how you relate to individuals— how many times you avoid someone, how much you talk and listen, how you feel in such encounters, what you think, and so on.

The purpose of this part of the exercise is for you to try to be as objective as possible about what you do, as well as the way you think and feel. In this way you will begin to understand more fully what you actually communicate not only in words but also in body language, facial expressions, and tone of voice.

4. *Now try to understand why you act in this manner.* Part of the reason grows out of the kind of individual you are—your pattern of strengths and the natural tendencies derived from your strengths. You may be naturally talkative or reluctant to speak. It may be easy for you to confront people honestly or it may be extremely difficult.

Sometimes, of course, you will find yourself acting contrary to your natural inclinations. For example, if I am highly motivated (feel very strongly) I speak more easily in a group, and the same is true if I feel quite secure. When I speak spontaneously in a larger group, however, I often worry about what I have said lest I have not said the proper thing or have been misunderstood.

On the other hand, talkative people sometimes remain silent. Some are well-disciplined and speak sparingly. Others may be inhibited by one or more group members, or they may simply not want to get involved. Perhaps they have learned that speaking on an issue often carries with it responsibility for doing something about it!

We also fall into temptations that grow out of the misuse of our strengths (or natural tendencies). Leadership ability, for example, may become domination. Natural shyness may lead to withdrawal. Self-confidence may become overconfidence or disdain for others. The ability to be a reconciler may lead to hesitation in risking the displeasure of those who disagree. Temptations have been discussed previously, and you will need to review what yours are as you seek to understand *why* you act in a particular way.

5. *Observe also how other people—especially those with whom you have problems—behave.* You may find as many examples of action you approve as those you disapprove. For example, there is a person with whom I have deliberately tried to build a better relationship. It has been easy for me to find behavior in him that irritates me. In a recent meeting I discovered that he was being a reconciler, a role he has not previously often fulfilled. Had I not been responsive to what he was doing, I might have missed this attempt on his part to change the way he usually acts in groups.

As you observe other people, you will need to be aware of their natural tendencies and their attempts to use these tendencies constructively, as well as the temptations which their inclinations lead them to express.

6. *Try to understand why they act in these ways.* You now apply to others the same objective analysis that you have previously used on yourself, in Step 4. You cannot be completely objective about others, of course, just as you

cannot be completely objective about yourself. As many
of the cases previously cited indicate, however, an attempt
to understand another person often leads to a change in
your own attitude toward that person.

You have now completed the process of analysis, and
we move on to your attempt to change your behavior. In
doing so you will need to follow the suggestions provided
in Chapters 7 and 8.

7. *Select a behavior that you want to exercise either in
a group or in relation to a group member outside.* In the
language of group dynamics, you are asked to *try out a
role* which you do not usually follow.

This proposed change must be as specific as you can
make it. It is not enough to say, "I want to stop dominating other family members." Rather, you must propose
some specific behavior: "I will not give my husband directions concerning how to reach our destination unless he
asks me." "I will speak five times in the meeting and say
nothing more unless I am asked for my opinion." "I will
ask for Mary's opinion and listen while she expresses it."

8. *Decide what steps you must take to accomplish your
goal.* For example, "reluctant speakers" may want to write
out what they plan to say ahead of time. "Ready speakers"
will hardly resort to taping their mouth shut literally, but
they will need something that works for them as effectively
as this physical inhibition of speech.

9. *Decide what you can do to make the group as a whole
more creative.* Once you have worked with regard to individuals, you are ready to tackle the group as a whole. For
example, I have found that some groups of which I am a
part require me to take more risks than are natural for me
just to move the group into action. On the other hand,
there are others where I can simply observe what is happening and know that the result will be creative without
much risk-taking on my part. Groups vary a great deal, and
even the same group will operate differently on different
occasions. One of the insights of group dynamics theory is

that all members must be sensitive to the tone and mood of a group before they will know what is required at a particular time.

10. *Keep evaluating both what you do and what is happening to the people involved.* Even small steps ahead are movements in the right direction. Groups are not usually remade overnight.

Improving Human Community

In this chapter we have been concerned with human community and what we can do to improve its quality. The examples used have pertained to staffs, marriage, and the family. The ideas are applicable to other collections of individuals trying to live or work together productively and creatively.

Human beings were made to live in such communal relationships. Genesis 2:18 sets the tone for human life: "It is not good that the man should be alone." It is equally true that it is not good for the woman to be alone. God has created humanity for community both with God and with one another.

For Christians, basic unity already exists in their oneness in Christ (Ephesians 4:4–6). We bring our own gifts to such community (Ephesians 4:11). Using these gifts creatively and "speaking the truth in love, we are to grow up in every way into him who is the head, into Christ, from whom the whole body, joined and knit together by every joint with which it is supplied, when each part is working properly, makes bodily growth and upbuilds itself in love" (Ephesians 4:15–16).

Discussion and Activity Guide

1. Choose either your work relationships or your family or both and work through the steps, beginning with No. 3, in "A Plan of Action." If desirable and feasible discuss this with the other people involved.

2. Think about and discuss with another person this question: What is my greatest need in improving my relationships with those with whom I live and work?

3. If you are already or want to become a religious person, consider whether the Bi/Polar System can offer you help in your relationship with God.

–10–

Claiming Your Future

I have said in a number of places that this is a "religious book" even though it does not often use "religious language." That is, it does not often speak of our relationship with God or our relationships with one another as they are affected by our belief in God. Nevertheless, I firmly believe that we have been dealing with religious thinking and the response of faith because of the *context* of the psychological principles and practices we have included. There are three major reasons why this is the case:

The first—and most basic—concern of the book has been that you are to understand, accept, and affirm your God-given strengths or gifts. This assertion pertains to who you are in relation to God's gifts to you in creation. *Celebrate who you are and who you were meant to be!* There is considerable agreement among persons of various religious beliefs about the importance of using God's gifts to us in the process of creation. Bi/Polar's basic premise is that the starting point for personal and social growth is to release the powers within us. To do so means that we are cooperating with God's creative process.

The second concern is that you learn to use these strengths or gifts to the fullest extent. That is, you are to learn how to allow God's creative strength to work through you in your inner (or personal) growth and in your outer (interpersonal, social) relationships. This concern is related to the doctrine of redemption, and there are wide variations of belief in how this occurs. What has been said in previous chapters, I believe, can be used within the context of most, if not all, particular understandings of God's way of working for our redemption. By redemption I mean God's activity within us to bring us to our full potential as his children in relation to himself and to one another.

The third primary concern is that you will be able to relate to others so as to build the kind of human community which provides a context for God's creative and redemptive power to work *through you*. The most common way by which the Divine Spirit works is through human community. We know God's love first as we experience human love, and we experience God's enabling power and love most often through our relationships with others. In turn we offer to God a channel through which his enabling love can be made real in the lives of other people.

These three concerns are captured in two picturesque terms used by Father John Powell in his book, *Why Am I Afraid to Tell You Who I Am?* He calls the first reality "interiority," which implies that a person has explored and experienced his/her identity. "He accepts who he is . . . (and) he knows that his potential self is even greater." [1] This concern is implemented through the identification of our particular strengths and the pattern those strengths form as the core (individuality) of our being.

"Exteriority," on the other hand, implies that a person "is open not only to himself but to his environment from without." [2] "Environment," of course, means partly other people, but Father Powell rightly recognizes that it consists of more than people and involves the entire range of God's creation.

---

[1] John Powell, *Why Am I Afraid to Tell You Who I Am?* (Niles, Illinois: Argus Communications, 1969), p. 32.
[2] *Ibid.*, p. 32 and ff.

The opposite of openness to our environment, Father Powell goes on to say, is "defensiveness." This is what we have called temptations to misuse our strengths so that we "hear" (experience) only what we want to experience.[3] That is, we are tempted to shape our little (or larger) world to *our* needs and wishes *alone* without listening to what other people and things have to say to us about the world beyond us.

This is, I believe, the central meaning of "original sin." Original sin, however we may interpret its inception, is to be distinguished from our sins—those of commission and omission (what we do and fail to do). Original sin is a condition or state of humanity which causes us to be tempted to focus on ourselves alone without appropriate reference to other people.

We do this in different, and often subtle, ways. Often the impression is given that only those who tend to be self-confident, with strong ego strength, fall into the temptation of self-centeredness. In Bi/Polar terms these are those with strong Independent Risking strength. But this is not the case at all.

People with higher Dependent Risking strength easily draw others to themselves for their own need even when they believe and give the impression of doing so for the sake of the other. A prime example is the self-sacrificing parent who makes his/her children overly dependent, often long after the children should be on their own.[4] I am personally aware of the temptation to perform acts of service to others out of my need to be considered "that good ole boy who never thinks of himself." The truth of the matter is that I am being quite self-centered in my efforts to manipulate others so that they will think well of me.

A variation of this latter theme, common to Patterns One and Three, is false humility, or "manipulative humility." The expression of this form of self-centeredness is

---

[3] *Ibid.*, p. 34.
[4] An example of this relationship of a mother and her children is found in the comic strip "Momma."

the attempt to create the impression, either openly or subtly, "Little ole me is not very important, and I just want to do the little things that I can to make the lives of others more pleasant."

I have known others whose goodness was just too obvious to be anything but repulsive, and this too is a kind of self-centeredness. These are the kinds of Christians who led Keith Miller to say, "I got sick of Christians." "Everywhere I went," he continues, "people were so 'good,' and so 'victorious.' They talked about their victories, and said, 'Give God the glory,' but the way they came across to me was, 'Look how good I am—with God's help, of course.'" [5] All patterns probably fall into this temptation, but Ones and Threes, and Fives and Sixes are most prone to do so.

Patterns Two and Four operate in their particular way to achieve the same end of self-centeredness, and it almost always involves for them a disdain for others, especially their practical or theoretical thought processes. Their temptation is to lose patience with others and to cut them off from any possibility of rectifying a mistake or improving in doing a piece of work.

Patterns Five and Six are tempted to overrelate, and either become too dependent or make others too dependent on them. What begins as a normal need for others or as the fulfilling of another's need escalates into a self-centeredness that manipulates others into meeting their own needs.

Patterns Seven and Eight are the classic examples of self-centeredness—"classic" only because of our tendency to identify a sense of self-confidence and power with self-centeredness. To be sure, they are always in danger of becoming self-centered but no more so than those who use humility, disdain, and people-manipulation as a way of self-gratification.

The paradox about which Father Powell and Miller

[5] Keith Miller, *The Becomers* (Waco, Texas: Word Book Publisher, 1973), p. 155.

write is the one we have tried to provide guidelines for in this book—the paradox of having to turn inward to move outward. Interiority and exteriority are two poles of the same bi/polar reality of life itself. The Parable of the Prodigal Son in Luke 15:11–32 provides the key to the new life that begins to deal creatively with the paradox: "But when *he came to himself* he said . . . I will arise and go to my father . . . ." This is what both psychology and religion recognize as the turning point for conversion or a new life: recognizing who we are (interiority) and moving toward something outside ourselves (exteriority). It is only when the alcoholic admits he is a drunk and needs a power greater than him/her self that the healing process begins. Or as the old saying puts it, "When it gets dark enough you can see the stars."

One of my frustrations in writing this book is that I have had to deal primarily with the first part of this paradox and only indirectly with the second. It is relatively easy through using the Bi/Polar System to provide you with new insights about yourself; it is much more difficult to provide the motivation to change. The power to change comes ultimately from God, but it is often transmitted to us by way of a person or a group, sometimes but less often by a piece of writing. Further, the power does not really work until it begins to flow through you to others. Members of Alcoholics Anonymous are wise in quickly encouraging one alcoholic to help another. Christian witness is not just a responsibility; it is also a way of increasing and renewing the Christian's faith.

Moreover, I have felt even more frustrated because I have not been able to provide you with the interpersonal relationship itself. The social nature of human life has led me to suggest in several places that you read this book with another person or a group. The chances of its proving to be really effective in your growth is greatly enhanced by this kind of interpersonal relationship.

How you secure this kind of group involvement will take

many different forms. Your own inclinations, the circumstances of your life, and many other factors will enter into your plan. But some kind of involvement with others is crucial.

As I have worked with Bi/Polar insights, I have repeatedly shared them in seminar groups; I have discussed them with colleagues also involved in the system; and I have talked about them with my wife. She has been my "sounding board" as I have written this book. Without this group involvement, this book would never have been written.

Your way of involving yourself with other people will not be the same as mine. Nor am I suggesting that you cannot benefit from the book alone. I am sure, however, that your benefit will be greater if you have the support and challenge of a group of two or more people to whom you in turn can be a channel of God's creative and redemptive power.

One thing is clear: you do not become a new person without struggle. I have said this in many ways throughout the book. Of course there is a time of "surrender"—when the alcoholic recognizes his/her inability to deal alone with the problem of alcohol or when the Christian pilgrim admits his/her utter dependence on God.

But that point in the pilgrimage is only a beginning. There is also struggle—the recognition of a failure and the need to try again and the development of the skill to live on a higher plane. Paul, who was as aware as any person of our inability to make it on our own, also wrote: "Work out your own salvation with fear and trembling" (Philippians 2:12).

The future that this struggle makes possible for you is a focus for your life. Through it you can become a centered self. By a centered self I mean two things.

The *essence* of the centered self is that your strengths are focused together to make it possible for you to realize your potentialities. You use your gifts—what you were given in creation—to serve the Creator. This is essentially the First Great Commandment: "You shall love the Lord your God with all your heart, and with all your soul, and with all your mind, and with all your strength" (Mark 12:30). It is also the first part of the Bi/Polar law of growth: Know, appreciate, and affirm who you are. You love God not with someone else's strengths but with your own—*your* heart, soul, mind, and strength. Those who are centered persons know who they are, what they can do, and how they can do it best. And they go on from there to use *all they are* in relation to the Creator God.

In other words you are called to love God with your whole being. In previous chapters I have tried to help you identify who you are and therefore how you are called to love God. This is the move toward effective interiority that involves self-understanding, self-acceptance, and self-affirmation.

This is only half of the process, however. The *expression* of the centered self is in relation to other people. Knowing who you are and affirming your identity make it possible for you to enter into creative and meaningful relationships. This is the second half of the Bi/Polar law of growth: use *all* your strengths in your human relationships. It is also the Second Great Commandment: "You shall love your neighbor as yourself" (Mark 12:31).

The opposite of the centered self is the polarized self. Centering involves all our strengths; polarization means using one or more without using others. The *self*-centered person is one who has become polarized on one strength at the expense of other strengths.

The purpose of this book has been to help you unblock the strengths you are not using so that you can get yourself together—to become a centered self rather than a self-centered one, able to love the neighbor as well as yourself by recognizing and dealing with the neighbor's needs.

Becoming a centered self involves struggle. The struggle

is partly against those forces which have held us down and kept us from being our best selves. It also involves the use of all our strengths or gifts more creatively for our own good and that of others.

There is no other way by which we can claim the future that God holds out for us but to accept it and then to work to make it real. The Letter of James is right; faith by itself is not enough, or as Paul would have put it, faith that is not expressed in behavior is no faith.

In this struggle there will be defeat and victory, travail and triumph, discouragement and joy, crucifixion and resurrection. God has provided us with gifts to be accepted and expressed, and in the struggle we are not alone. In that strength we can go on.

Discussion and Activity Guide

1. Look at the goals you were asked to formulate after reading Chapter 1. Have you made progress in accomplishing them? If the Bi/Polar System was not helpful in regard to those particular goals, where else can you go for help?

2. If this book has led you to believe that you need a deeper kind of help than it provides, consider seeing your priest, rabbi, or pastor, or go to a professional counselor. In most cities there are professionals where you are charged according to your income. They will be associated with either publicly supported or private agencies engaged in the helping professions.

Appendix

Tendencies and Temptations [1]

Tendencies are the way we are disposed to think, feel, and behave because of our strengths, and these tendencies are good. Temptations, on the other hand, are the misuse of our strengths or the result of becoming polarized on some strength, so that the strength is expressed in a destructive manner. In your move toward self-understanding and a knowledge of how you need to change, circle the numbers of those temptations to which you either occasionally or often succumb.

Tendencies and Temptations Related to Bi/Polar Thinking and Bi/Polar Risking

The *tendency* is to:

1. Emphasize the importance of reason. [2]
2. Experience a high drive to accomplish.

The *temptation* is to:

1. Regard reason as more valuable than emotion. [2]
2. Be impatient.

---

[1] J. W. Thomas, *Bi/Polar: A Positive Way of Understanding People* (Richardson, Texas: BI/POLAR, Incorporated, 1978), pp. 112, 120, 134. Used by permission.

[2] Odd numbered tendencies and temptations are more likely to be characteristic of those stronger in Thinking, even numbered of those stronger in Risking.

3. Be rational and objective.

4. Want others to get into action.
5. Approach a situation calmly and rationally.
6. Experience strong feelings.
7. Make decisions through rational analysis
8. Make the decision in spite of the risk.
9. Rely primarily on my thinking to solve my problems.
10. Experience compassion for others.
11. Think carefully before making a decision.
12. Emphasize the importance of feelings.
13. Solve my problems with thinking.
14. Solve my problems by taking action.

3. Treat my emotions as something that need to be kept under control and not expressed.
4. Press others to decide quickly.
5. Hide my feelings.

6. Act on impulse alone.

7. Disregard my intuition.

8. Make the decision too quickly.
9. Regard what I think as more important than how I feel.
10. Let my heart rule my reason.
11. Procrastinate in making decisions.
12. Regard feelings as more important than reason.
13. Solve my problems with thinking alone.
14. Solve my problems with action alone.

Tendencies and Temptations Related to Practical and Theoretical Thinking

The *tendency* is to:
15. Emphasize the importance of facts.[3]
16. Speculate about how things could be.

17. Follow established procedures.

The *temptation* is to:
15. Treat facts as more important than ideas.[3]
16. Keep on speculating when it is time to be getting the facts.
17. Cling to established procedures.

[3] Odd numbered tendencies and temptations are more likely to be characteristic of those stronger in Practical Thinking, even numbered of those stronger in Theoretical Thinking.

18. Imagine the possibilities.

18. Let what I imagine become a substitute for reality.

19. Be consistent.

19. Resist change.

20. Enjoy thinking about ideas.

20. Think about ideas so much that the practical side of life is neglected.

21. Think about problems.

21. Keep on thinking about problems when I should be thinking about possible solutions.

22. Emphasize the importance of ideas.

22. Regard ideas as more important than facts.

23. Get the facts.

23. Use facts as clubs to destroy ideas.

24. Want to communicate ideas.

24. Overkill an idea by restating it over and over again.

25. Be realistic about myself.

25. Think negatively about myself.

26. Consider the alternatives.

26. Stay so busy considering the alternatives that I never make a decision.

27. Recognize the dangers and pitfalls in a situation.

27. Become discouraged and depressed.

28. Appreciate the value of ideas.

28. Treat ideas as more important than their practical application.

Tendencies and Temptations Related to Dependent and Independent Risking

The *tendency* is to:

The *temptation* is to:

29. Accept the reality of my own [4] faults and weaknesses.

29. Underestimate my own strengths.[4]

30. Feel self-confident.

30. Use my self-confidence to depend less on other people.

---

[4] Odd number tendencies and temptations are more likely to be characteristic of those stronger in Dependent Risking, even numbered of those stronger in Independent Risking.

31. Be accommodating and agreeable.
32. Feel personally responsible.
33. Pay attention to the feelings and thoughts of others.

34. Depend on myself.

35. Want to please others.

36. Express my thoughts and feelings.

37. Be understanding of other people's mistakes.

38. Talk easily and freely.

39. Appreciate others in a group.
40. Enjoy being alone.

41. Respect others.

42. Have high drive to influence others.

43. Be quiet and listen.

44. Want to keep my independence in relationships.

31. Say "yes" when I should say "no."
32. Take on more than I can handle.
33. Avoid confrontation and conflict by not expressing my own thoughts and feelings.
34. Do it myself rather than ask for help.
35. Go overboard in trying to please everyone.
36. Be overly aggressive in expressing my thoughts and feelings.
37. Make excuses for other people's mistakes; attempt to whitewash their faults.
38. Talk too much and not listen enough.
39. Underrate myself in a group.
40. Withdraw from involvement with other people.
41. Allow others to take advantage of me without saying anything.
42. Think about what I am going to say rather than listen to what is being said.
43. Listen too much and not speak up when I should.
44. Hold people at arm's length.